Nail It In 90 for Direct Selling & Network Marketing

Kim Johnson & Alice Hinckley

ISBN-13: 978-0692657096
ISBN-10: 0692657096

Kim
To all of my coaching clients who keep my on purpose & driven to live at the next level...I would not be the person I am without all of you!

Alice
To all of the network marketing professionals who have impacted my life over the years as team members, mentors and friends.
Grateful to you for helping me learn so many valuable lessons to share with others on our path to success.

Table of contents

Welcome - from Kim

I am so happy you have made the choice to join Nail It In 90!
Nothing is more satisfying than setting a goal and making it happen.
Nail It In 90 has been designed to have you take this process and condense it into a systematic way of achieving your outcome.

After spending nearly 20 years in the self-development industry, traveling the world, and coaching thousands of people, I came to the realization that 90 days of focus really is the best way to achieve what you want. It is not a quick fix. It is not always easy. It is ALWAYS amazingly satisfying when you are done. I used this process to create my original Nail It In 90 book, complete a workout program, and relocate our family from Rhode Island to South Carolina, all within the SAME 90 days. It has become my go to methodology...BECAUSE IT WORKS. As I have incorporated this technique with my private coaching clients, the success rates of accomplishments have jumped dramatically. I have even gone so far as to have clients texting me intentions and results daily. All for outstanding results.

Part of my motivation for this work is to be able to reach those who need it most, the people who could not spend enormous amounts of money on coaching and seminars. I wanted anyone to be able to buy this book on a random Friday evening, devour the content, get clear on their outcomes over the weekend, and start on Monday.
Simple. Easy. Productive.

So let's get going and change your life!

Welcome - from Alice

Goal setting has always been a part of my adult life. Yes, I have an achiever personality. What I have learned in over twenty years as an entrepreneur is consistent effort over a long period of time produces lasting results. Whenever I set a goal, I always break it down into bite-size chunks, so I know what needs to be done every day, week and month to accomplish my goals.

Kim's "Nail It In 90" process is a focused way of achieving a goal or outcome. It takes the steps I have done over and over to achieve success personally and professionally and leads you day by day to your outcome.

Having achieved success in both corporate sales and with two different direct selling companies, it is my passion to help others find the success their heart desires. Partnering with Kim to tailor the Nail It In 90 process for direct sales/network marketing makes perfect sense to me. A key to success in network marketing is consistent, persistent effort over time. Focusing on a goal in your business for 90 days will create the momentum you need to promote in the compensation plan, create explosive growth in your team, achieve the criteria for that amazing incentive trip, move your income to the six-figure category and so much more.

Let's partner together to help you reach that next step in ultimate success in the direct selling industry.

Invisible threads are the strongest ties.
- Friedrich Nietzsche

What Can You Expect?

Everything you need to be successful is within this book and within your heart. If you take both and mix with immediate action, you will see and experience changes in yourself and your life. The power lies within you.

This book is set up to act as your workbook & journal to record your progress and thoughts as we go. It is a wonderful tool to look back upon when you are on day ninety and beyond. We also have log pages on our website that you can download to keep track of your process.

If you would like to join us for additional support and coaching beyond this book, we have created audio programs available for purchase geared towards specific subjects.

If you still feel you need even more personalized connection, we are available for private coaching on a limited basis.

All of the information about additional programs can be located by visiting our website at www.NailItIn90.com.

Now you know everything we have to offer! No up-selling. No secrets. No feeling left out. You can participate as you see fit.

Your adventure is about to begin!

Working The NII90 Day Process

My husband often reminds me, "The road to disappointment is paved with missed expectations." It always sounds funny to me when he says it.

I am sure that is because I build up most things to be much more dramatic in my mind!

In order to be consistently on the same page, I want you to know what to expect; so here you go!

1. This is not a cake walk; it will require you to be here with us each and every day.

2. Rome wasn't built in a day, nor will your successes be built in a day.

3. You are about to become the tortoise, not the hare. In the end, constant effort always wins.

4. We will provide you with mindset strategies and distinctions.

5. You will provide the daily actions that will build upon each other, no matter what your project may be.

6. Execution is the name of this game. The more we execute on beliefs with actions towards the goals, the greater the results.

7. Throughout the book, you will be asked questions. Answer them immediately. Do so without your filters, being as honest as you can. Being honest with yourself is the key to success in NII90.

8. Whatever aspect of your business you have chosen to work on for the next 90 days, make sure you are passionate about completing it! It must bring joy to your very being just thinking about completing it. Your intention and excitement matter immensely when it comes to actual results.

9. Frustration will happen. So what!!!! Keep going no matter what!

10. Day 90 will come whether you give it your all or not. We suggest you give it your "all." You can't imagine the feeling of pride you will experience just by completing 90 straight days of simple actions towards a deeply desired outcome.

One Simple Action

Simplicity. The ever elusive element we seek in our lives. You may have started your business because you believed by doing so, you would ultimately create an easier life for yourself. Residual income, connection with people or adding to your current monthly income likely played a part in your decision to enter into network marketing. Remembering the reason you started your business is not always enough to be successful in your business. In fact, most people have a very hard time sticking with their business because they immediately become overwhelmed. With all good intent, we grab on to all the information offered to us when we start with a new company, ready to dive in with 1000% commitment. And quickly, we are overwhelmed with information about the products, the learning material, sales material and the list goes on and on.

Before we know it, the original enthusiasm we felt has slowed down or stopped. Overwhelm is taking control, leaving us not sure why we even started this! Now's the time to breathe and realize there is a way to manage all this; one simple action at a time. Rather than trying to be successful immediately, realize true success is a step-by-step process. Every step counts towards your success, no matter how seemingly small the step may be. We all have very busy lives; that is not debatable in today's society. We are overstimulated, over-committed, overtired and overwhelmed.

The only way to combat this is to simplify. This does not mean to sell everything you own and go live in a tiny house, unless, of course, that's what you want. What it does mean is recognize that one step at a time, while focusing on one specific item at a time, is the key to success. Each step, each piece, adds to the overall success of the goal.

The very first step of our 90 day journey together begins with you agreeing each step you take matters, no matter how small it seems. Focus on the "win" of completing even the simplest of tasks.

one simple
thing everyday
can change
your world

Why Are You Part of Direct Selling/Network Marketing?

What caused you to begin a business in the direct selling/network marketing industry? Did you fall in love with your company's product and realize you had to help share its impact with others? Did you respect the person who showed you the opportunity and believed you could build a business too? Did you join because you need money? Did you commit to this path for creating a better lifestyle for your family? Did you get involved because you were attracted to the positive attitude of the people you met? Do you know someone who has been successful in network marketing and thought if they could do it then so could you?

Every entrepreneur must determine why making their business an extraordinary success is important to them. What is your motivation to be successful? Do you have a crazy passion to change the trajectory of wellness in your country or city? Are you driven to help others change from a mindset of poverty to abundance? Did you grow up wanting for food or always wearing hand-me-down clothes or watching your parents fight about money? Now you have promised yourself no one in your family will have to overcome those experiences.

It is vital to have a crystal clear definition of why you must succeed in your business. If your goal is "fluffy" like making more money, when times get difficult, you will quit. The ultimate key to success in this industry is to find the company that is your ideal fit, take action on your business every day, and never, ever, ever give up!

How do you discover the attachment to "why I must succeed?" It is all about finding a compelling reason and determining "what emotion" achieving that reason will produce for you. For example, if your goal is to have the funds to pay for your child's education so they can graduate debt-free and move into their career without burden, it's not just about the money to pay the tuition and expenses. Truly, the emotions you are going to experience are the real success. Imagine the pride as a parent of watching your child walk across the stage and receive the diploma. Grasp the sense of relief you feel knowing they go out into the world unburdened by debt. Settle into the sense of contribution you feel for being the best parent you could be for your child.

Let's get clear on the emotions you are seeking to experience by succeeding in your network marketing business. Close your eyes, and take a deep breath. It's likely you have already set goals or imagined the level of success you starve to experience. Now, ask yourself how you will feel when you achieve that goal. What emotions run through you as you share with another the success you have achieved through diligent progress toward a goal?

Each of us will have our own feelings on reaching the goal and achieving success. Are you relieved? Exhilarated? Humbled? Gleeful? Proud? Tearful? Excited? Jubilant? Satisfied? Grateful? Appreciative? Hungry for more? Allow your body to feel the experience. You want to have these intense emotions to draw on when the road to success has twists and turns.

Jot a few notes for yourself. Describe the feelings. What will you experience when your goal becomes a reality? Feel it in every cell of your body.

What Is Your Definition Of Success?

Whether you are aware of it or not, you have a definition of success. Actually, we have definitions for most of the elements of our life. For example, you have an internal definition of what it means to look great when you're getting ready to go out. You also have a definition of what it means to look sloppy when you come home from the gym! As human beings, we have definitions for love, fear, intelligence,beauty… the list goes on and on. If you are unaware of your definition for a specific area of your life, you'll never know how you're achieving it or how you're failing it. The tricky part comes when you are working wholly unaware you even a definition for something and are responding to an unconscious guide deep within yourself.

I don't know about you, but when I was growing up no one ever asked me what my definition of love was, or for that matter success. Most of us have created our internal definitions based on how we were raised, the people we were exposed to, and through pain and pleasure. If you experienced success early on in your life, let's say with sports, and everyone was cheering for you, there is a strong probability you imprinted what that version of success meant. This most likely served you very well throughout your sports career. However, there is a strong probability, that when people don't cheer for you in other areas of your life you experience sadness or frustration. All because of something that happened when you hit a home run or scored points when you were ten years old!

It's my opinion, until you understand your internal definitions and rules for life, you will find yourself running into unexpected unhappiness and missed expectations. Make no mistake about it, this runs deep within us as human beings. Most of the definitions I'm speaking about were imprinted upon you when you were young. That, however, does not leave us without responsibility for choosing to keep them as adults. One of the most resourceful things I ever experienced in my life was the understanding that I can choose what I believe about something or someone. Entering into a state of mindfulness and asking these questions, allows you to live at a much higher level emotionally. The idea being when you know better, you can do better.

Discovering my personal definition of success was not a direct course. At the time, I had no idea about the power of questions. All I knew was I wanted to be successful. I was not even sure I was doing what I really loved in life, but I knew I had to make money and be successful. The very first time I started asking these questions with the intent of discovery, I realized I was completely clueless. For me, success seems to be hardwired to time and creativity, not money. Yet all I was doing was chasing money. My levels of unhappiness were at an all-time high. I had lots of money, very little time, and zero creativity in my life. This led to anxiety attacks and my stress was off the charts. Because I was out of ideas, I decided to do some deep self-development to find my answers. The questions I asked myself led me to a deep understanding of my personal definition of success.

No two definitions are the same. Much like fingerprints are unique; definitions can have many twists and curves. Discovering your definition requires patience and curiosity. It requires a heightened sense of awareness to pay attention to the unique and slight shifts in emotions. Above all, it requires you decide to listen to even the slightest whisper in your mind with a twinge in your stomach. I have always found these signals are probably the strongest clues we as human beings have in defining our true definitions. Remember, it's very easy to deny all of the little nuances you'll feel in this process. It's very easy to gloss over the emotions, dismissing them like you would have a slight breeze. The key to success lies in your willingness to explore your inner thoughts and feelings.

So what is the difference between a want and a need? Understanding your definitions in any area of your life requires you to understand the difference between wants and needs. Many, many, many times, we confuse the two. I may think I need to have an entire list of items met to be successful when in fact, only one or two are in actual need. The rest are in fact wants. Often wants are not acknowledged because we believe a need sounds better than a want. This level of honesty with yourself will make you uncomfortable. People give up at this point because they just can't face their true feelings. It's only through the discovery of the definitions that you can live on the other side identifying your wants and needs. Unfortunately, I've never found a long-lasting solution that did not involve this level of self-awareness. My many years of coaching others as well as having a coach myself, have made it indisputably clear the necessary work to reach the other side.

What have your past definitions of success been telling you? Capture all of the past definitions of success you have been living by, and how they showed up in your results.

Now that you see what your past definitions of success have been and how they have affected your life, it's time to see what a new definition, designed with intention, will bring forward in your life. See yourself as successful, achieving and being as you would want yourself to be in twelve months from now. Experience this image with as much detail as possible using all of your senses to complete the vision. When you have defined a clear perspective, ask yourself what does this definition of success look like?

What is your new version of success?

Once you have clarified your new definition of success, it's important to understand exactly how you know when you're experiencing success. Some people have such complicated definitions they are never clear on when they are actually experiencing success. Understanding what makes you feel think and see success in your moment to moment and day-to-day life, allows you to experience success as many times as you choose per day. You see, you are in charge of all the rules, the great rules as well as the bad rules. Make sure you understand how you experience success.

How do you know when you are experiencing success?

Are You A Leader Or A Follower?

Leadership by definition is the act of guiding or directing others in a group. This definition seems so basic. In this case, a leader would be anyone who gives orders or instructions to a group who is required to follow those instructions. From my experience, leadership ultimately boils down to influence. Influence is being a compelling force which effects the actions, behaviors and opinions or others.

Technically, you can be considered a leader because of a title you are given. In reality, you are only a leader if people are following you. A leader in action works on their skills of influence. A leader is always seeking ways to upgrade their communication with individuals and groups.

Dr. John C. Maxwell, world renowned leadership expert, wrote, "Leadership is not about titles, positions or flowcharts. It is about one life influencing another."

Do you consider yourself a leader? Do you default to being a follower? Do you sometimes choose to be a follower? One trait of a remarkable leader is to know when to lead and when to follow. If you say yes to leading in every area of your life, some of the leadership positions you take on may not get your best effort. Learning to say no is a highly practiced skill of exceptional leaders.

One of the main goals of leaders is to raise up other leaders. In the direct selling industry, over-the-top success is achieved by leaders who learn to raise up other leaders. The entire premise of the industry is to have lots of people producing instead of one person doing all the production. The only way to develop a massive team is to continually teach people how to lead within your company. Empower them to teach training. Encourage them to lead conference calls. Coach them on motivating their new team members. The more leaders you promote, the more successful your business.

For example, allowing another person to take the lead conducting a meeting, hosting a conference call or organizing an event is on-the-job training for raising up a leader. Mentor them on what to say. Remind them to practice so they are natural. Let go. Will they be perfect? Probably not. You aren't always perfect. Growing leaders is about instilling confidence. After you have encouraged someone to take a leadership role in a meeting, on a call or with their growing team, then be sure to debrief with them. What did they experience? What was so strong they want to make sure they build on it? What area was a bit shaky for them? How can they practice and improve in that area? What skills can they improve so next time it feels like even more of a success for them?

This process can be summarized as *Plan-Do-Review.* Plan what role the person will take at an event or on a call. Let them do it. Then review the results and make adjustments for future improvement.

What must you do to continue to develop yourself as a leader? Identify the character traits of leaders you admire. Purpose to develop those traits within yourself. Here are some of the character traits we look for in great leaders: Strong Communicator. Active Listener. Committed. Integrity. Compassionate. Inspiring. Authentic. Trustworthy. Honest. Centered. Happy. Goal-oriented. Confident. Positive. Empowering. Flexible. Persuasive. Positive. Risk-taker. Focused. Optimistic. Decisive. Influential.

List the traits of a great leader you intend to develop:

What Does Money Mean To You?

Money is a physical coin, paper or plastic for the purpose of purchasing goods and services. However, the idea of money and the impact it has on our feelings and behaviors goes way beyond the physical aspect of having money in your wallet.

We all have beliefs and emotions related to money. These can be complex and the underlying reason why we do or don't have the wealth we say we desire. Our beliefs around money are based on what we observed growing up, on experiences we went through, and on what we were taught by our family. These observations, teachings and experiences are reflected in our current financial behaviors.

Being aware of your current beliefs around money will allow you to let go of the old story, if it is not serving you, and build a new story around money. Let's consider the question, "What is money?" Take the time to come up with at least ten responses to the question. Dig deep. Peel back the layers. Write it down.

What is money?

What is money?

What is money?

What is money?

What is money?

What is money?

What is money?

What is money?

What is money?

What is money?

Consider your answers. What shift can you make that will help money flow
to you more easily? Some people use money as a measure of their value or
self-worth. Money is often a point of conflict in relationships. What will you
do to develop a healthier attitude toward money?

My belief is money is energy and there is always more than enough. When I shifted to this belief years ago, it altered the course of my financial wealth because I started making different decisions. Growing up I always heard money didn't grow on trees. Making a decision to start respecting all the money I earned and embracing prosperity allowed my businesses to flourish.

Another aspect of money you will find crucial to your success is giving back. Embrace the concept of charitable giving or tithing. If you give back to areas where you receive your personal growth, you become a catalyst to money flowing freely. Those who choose to hold tight to every penny keep the flow from happening. To give you an idea how I donate to areas that have helped me grow, let me share a specific example. I attended the eWomen National Conference in Dallas last fall. I learned so much to help my business. Shawn Achor, author of The Happiness Advantage, impacted me deeply with his research on happiness in the workplace. Because of the person I became while attending the conference, I made the decision to donate to the eWomen Foundation. The eWomen Foundation gives to many charities to assist women and children throughout North America. Who has impacted your life for the better? Do they have a cause you believe in? Give back. Keep the money flowing.

What Will Prevent You From Completing 90 Days?

When I put this question in the original Nail It In 90 book, I was constantly asked: "why would you want us to think about what we are doing wrong?" Surprisingly, people had a very strong reaction to the mere thought of failure. However, without the understanding of failure, you cannot succeed. You MUST consciously acknowledge what your potential roadblocks are before you even begin.

Truth be told, you already know before we start if you will finish.
Now STOP. THINK ABOUT THAT FOR A MOMENT.
You already know whether you will succeed with your 90 days.

When we make decisions and choices to do something, we already know in our gut whether or not we will actually do it. We understand our level of commitment immediately. Some will argue they really, really wanted it and they just couldn't make it happen. They did everything possible. They tried their best. I will stand firm in my position that when you make a decision to do it, you will move mountains to see it through. You will seek help. You will work hard. You will research and MAKE IT HAPPEN. THIS IS CONVICTION. Without conviction, you will allow circumstances to get in your way and clutter your path. If you pause for a moment and think of the times in your life when you JUST KNEW you would make something happen, you will see the difference. That difference, that distinction is everything. It is the gap between success and failure.

I'm sure you all know direct selling and network marketing can be challenging! Experiencing rejection is a regular part of owning your own network marketing business. No matter how glamorous someone may have indicated this business is, it's hard work with lots of rejection. And there's no way around it. So as you're here, contemplating what will prevent you from completing this 90 days, rejection will be a part of it. If you're thinking to yourself right now, "the rejection factor is the thing that scares me most," I applaud you for being honest. Just knowing this is your biggest and most fearful roadblock, can help us overcome it. Sometimes by simply acknowledging something is there, it's no longer quite as scary as it once was. That's not to say this will be easy. Remember at the beginning of this book I said it's not an easy process, simple but not easy. It has been my experience, however, understanding your roadblocks is the key to overriding fear and creating unprecedented success.

Pause for a moment, take a deep breath and prepare, to be honest.
So I am asking you, challenging you, to make the choice right here, right now.
Will you do what it takes to make your outcome happen? Are you willing to look at what will stop you, so you can strategize how it won't affect you when it does show up? Are you prepared for the rejection that is certain to come your way over the next 90 days? Could you even welcome the rejection, believing every no is one step closer to YES? What would happen if you just decided to be yourself, relax, and know that the people you are supposed to enroll in your downline are simply waiting for you to find them? What would happen if you simply decided to give as much attention to your positive thoughts as you do your negative thoughts?

These are the moments that define your true intent. Make a choice for yourself. Be honest right now. YOU KNOW. Create a conviction. You will finish, NO MATTER WHAT.

Now capture everything you can think of that will be a roadblock to reaching your goal. Even the smallest, the minutest of fear, can stop you. However only if you let them. Write down everything you can think of that scares you, causes you to pause and sets you astray from the path of completing your outcomes. Remember, even the smallest of small thoughts go down so they cannot blindside you.

If you acknowledge them, write them down and recognize them when they show up, you overcome them. It's that simple.

What has stopped you in the past from completing your goals?

What will prevent you from completing this 90 day goal?

What Is On Your Annoying List?

We all have annoying things in our lives, the leaky faucet, the rug that never sits just right and trips us daily, a cabinet door that never closes, plants that need to be repotted, Christmas lights that are still up in March, a bunch of socks without their match.

Our proverbial annoying list. The running list we internalize of items that irritate us, yet we put up with them! When you have a list of things that annoy you, they clutter your energy. They block progress and creativity. They hang you up every day and you know it. Every year my husband and I go through our lives and make an annoying list to fix what gets in our way.

My nemesis...LEGOS. My son and the Legos. They were EVERYWHERE. It only takes stepping on a lost Lego in the carpet once to realize you never want to do it again. I put this annoyance on my list a few years ago. My husband had a genius way of solving this. A king size white sheet with ALL the Legos in the middle. Simply unfold the sheet on the floor when you want to play and fold it back up when you are done. AMAZING. Annoyance gone.

Most of the time the annoying items eat up time and energy causing us to take away time from what we really want to be doing. Worst of all, they send us down the road of aggravation leaving us in a less than desirable mood for our day. Think about how much time is wasted, preventing you from using this precious time on your business! You see, direct selling and network marketing businesses are part of your everyday life. When your everyday life has things in it that are not working for you, they are a huge time suck, preventing you with making the connections that are part of every direct seller's business. If you are spending your time looking for lost files, car keys, and trying to manage your family's chaos, you are wasting time. By handling all of the "annoying" items, you will gain time.

Solution: make your annoying list below IMMEDIATELY.

Know what you need to fix to move on in your life. I promise you, once you make the list and work your way through the items, piece by piece, you will feel liberated! Even if it requires hiring people to help such as an organizer or a skilled technician for the things you personally can't fix, it is worth every penny. While it may take you a week to work through your annoying list, you won't have to do it for the next six months. Handle things as they show up one at a time and you'll never have to do it again.

Where Is Your Urgency?

Urgency. It can be a friend or a foe. When you live in a state of urgency day to day, it is definitely your foe. It will burn out your adrenal glands, make you short tempered, and cause you to act as if you don't know yourself at all.

However, when used with a light touch, it can be the sparkle added to motivation. Just as you finish a wonderfully prepared soup with a pinch of salt, the flavor bursts into life.

Using urgency in your mindset is no different. If you have a flash of divine clarity that you have been complacent, far too long, urgency can make your butt move!

However, you must know what is driving your urgency. We all have reasons why we want to make things happen. It is my experience there is a deeper, more finite reason called urgency that resides in your gut. It's the voice that says "If not now, when?". It's the knowing you turned 30, 50, 65 and you are still not where you wanted to be by this momentous occasion. It could simply be you have just had enough of yourself. The excuses, the behavior, the lack of progress up until this moment. Whatever it is, it's urgency. Maybe somewhere in the back of your mind when you signed up for your network marketing business, you had a sense of urgency. You thought to yourself, "if they can do it I can do it" and you truly believed it. But somehow, in the day-to-day working of the business, you have forgotten your urgency you have forgotten the entire reason you started this to begin with. Most people do. When I ask my clients to give me their number one reason they enrolled with the company they are working with, quite often there is a pause, and then they will tell me about how fantastic the product is. The product being fantastic is not enough. Knowing why you are there and what brought you there in the first place, is the difference between success and failure. In the final analysis, urgency is like spice to me. When used in the right amounts the dishes are amazing. Use too much, and the dish is in the garbage disposal. Use too little, and the meal was nothing to remember.

So the question is, "Where is your urgency?". Capture all of your "urgency" below.

What Do You Need to Thrive as a Direct Selling or Network Marketing Professional?

Are you thriving in your business or are you just surviving? Over and over again people refer to network marketing as a personal development program with a compensation plan. One thing for sure, choosing the path of a professional in direct selling or network marketing will be a learning experience. Thriving in your business is not just about creating an income. Thriving is often about making a difference. Thriving will be defined differently for each person. We must each take the time to ask ourselves, "What has to happen for me to thrive in my business?"

Thriving in my business—what really juices me—is to see the excitement and awe in others when they accomplish a goal. Maybe it's a promotion or reaching a certain sales level. Maybe it is earning an incentive trip or being recognized on the stage at the annual convention for your accomplishments. For me, asking my team members their goals, helping them create a plan to reach or surpass the goal, and then cheering and assisting them to success, this is truly thriving as a network marketing professional.

We don't often ask ourselves these types of questions. Thriving is being prosperous or successful. Thriving is flourishing. Thriving is growing or developing vigorously. Time to let your imagination go wild!

WHAT HAS TO HAPPEN FOR YOU TO THRIVE? Capture everything and anything you can. Make sure you keep yourself in a positive mindset while you are doing this exercise! Make it a specific point not to allow any of your negative self-talk to take over.

You have determined what it means for you to thrive. Now is the time to consider how you can weave small actions into your life each and every day to thrive. Remember, it is all about starting. Start now and take small, positive steps forward. You will look back in a few months and realize you now thrive in your life all the time.

What Story Are You Living?

Everyone has a story. From the moment we wake up until the moment we go to sleep, we are telling ourselves stories in our mind. Your day, your business, your life, are a direct reflection of the stories you tell. The interesting thing about stories is some of them are not true. We sit down to watch a movie, most of the time we know if this is a true story or fiction we are watching. It's a useful tool in our appreciation of the movie. Funny thing is, though, we don't ask ourselves that same question about the stories that go on in our mind! For some reason, on some level, we believe what we think. Whether it's true or not is completely irrelevant. This is why your personal story is so important to your outcome.

If you have a story you don't have time for your business, you will not have time for your business. If you have a story that finding new clients is hard, you will have a hard time finding clients. What's even more interesting, is the fact that most of our stories are negatively framed. The story leaves us filled with doubt and anguish, constantly wondering if we've made the right choices and questioning our next move. The truth is human beings are hardwired here to protect us. When left unchecked, that fear becomes doubt. We begin to question everything we're doing, making little to no progress. While we need fear to protect us in our daily lives, we certainly don't need it to protect us from making progress.

No matter what business you are in, you must decide what your story will be. This comes back to being a leader or a follower. Leaders make up their story, do what it takes to make it happen and live it. Followers, on the other hand, are the people who support the leader's dreams. Each step forward in the role of a follower allows the leader's vision to materialize. It's great if you have a common vision, it's a nightmare if it's not where you want to be. You can easily use someone else's story to determine what your story will be; this is the power of modeling. If your up-line has an outstanding attitude and a beautiful way of influencing people into using the products and/or enrolling in the business, it will benefit you greatly to model their behavior. However that being said, it must be a story you feel is true to you as well. If you feel you are forcing yourself into that story, then it will never work.

Let me give you a great example. I do personal coaching with people. Typically, the rules around personal coaching are very strict. Most coaches do not allow time in between sessions for conversations and/or e-mails without charging. They are constantly worried about being paid for their time. This felt very foreign to me. If I was going to be someone's coach, and be their outstanding coach, then why would I not want to know what was going on within and between sessions and help them if they were stuck? Early on in my career, I adopted a practice of allowing my clients to text me, call me and/or e-mail me whenever they felt stuck, overwhelmed, or simply wanted to celebrate. I've had more than one seasoned coach tell me this was a mistake. I wouldn't be able to handle the number of people that became "needy" and took up my time without regard for it. None of this changed my mind. I did what I knew I had to do for me to be happy in this business. I wrote my own story. I said my clients will use it gingerly. I said my clients understand this is a privilege not to be abused. I am happy to report not once, not even once, have I had to have the uncomfortable conversation with somebody about taking advantage of my kindness. I wrote my own story.

What is your story about your business? How do you see your business? How do you see you showing up in your business? The lines are blank, and the ideas are wide open. Be brave and write the story of a leader; your story.

The Art & Science Of Connection

What is Networking? Networking is connection. We network in almost every activity during the day. Instead of thinking of networking as a business activity you go out to do to generate leads, consider networking a lifestyle where you become an influential connector.

The basic principal of being a successful networker is authenticity. Be yourself. Decide which values are most important in your life and live them with your words and actions. For example, if integrity is important to you in your business, then always speak truth. No little white lies allowed. You must be honest and open to be considered a person of integrity. Always speak highly of others or say nothing at all. Think about it. What three character traits or values do you want to shine through in every interaction you have with another person? Compassion. Intelligence. Honesty. Loyalty. Friendly. Strong. Faithful. Committed. Happy. Helpful. Generous. Genuine. Trustworthy. Remember you are unique. Choose the traits that are your strengths and live by them. Showing your true self to others will enable them to connect with you more quickly and feel strong about the connection.

View every human interaction as networking. Going to a business meeting to encounter prospects is, of course, networking. However, attending recreational or social events are also examples of networking opportunities.

In society today, many people are realizing the need to start their own business and not be so dependent on corporate America.   Therefore, we find many people venturing into network marketing who have not had any experience in the marketplace except as an employee. If you are one of those people, let's take time to examine how you want to present yourself in networking opportunities.

In order to weave being a connector and influencer into your life, so you network naturally, it is vital to be confident in presenting your business to others in a concise manner. In other words, create your networking identity so whether you are at an official business networking event, at a church social, at your child's soccer game, or meeting a new neighbor, you can confidently share your passion for your business and have them curious and wanting to know more.

You want to feel as natural sharing your business as you do talking about your adorable kids or your fun little dog. The more you talk to people, the more comfortable you will be.

Do you consider yourself a master networker? If the answer is yes, terrific! Take those skills out into the world today and start connecting with new people. If your answer is no, then let's take a moment to consider the characteristics of a master networker. First of all, master networkers have the belief they have something to offer everyone they meet. This doesn't mean every person they meet wants to buy the product or service of their network marketing company. It does mean they believe they can offer a connection or an insight to help each person they meet. Maybe they can recommend a group or a book or a person who can help them. Master networkers are all about establishing relationships. They realize when they put others first, as time goes on, those people reach out to them too.

What is the physiology of a master networker? They hold their shoulders back. They smile. They ask questions and actively listen to the answers. They look people in the eye when they talk to them. They are attentive and genuine. They keep their body language open. Master networkers literally make sure their heart is facing the person they are talking to at any moment. Their physiology includes nodding in agreement. What does your physiology when you meet new people say about you? Are you excited to get to know them or scared they will reject you? You are sending non-verbal messages with your body language all the time. Be sure your physical message is congruent with your words.

We will examine the art and science of connection and becoming a master networker in more detail during our 90 days together. Let's start with asking yourself, what must happen for you to become a master networker?

Jot down a few notes to reflect on.

Living A Purposeful Mindset

Setbacks will show up. As I stated earlier, if you are committed to making your business a success, you will find the way. The question is whether or not you do experiencing overwhelm or happiness. Living and creating with the understanding of your personal happiness is your choice. Choice is powerful. Action fuels it. There are some very simple distinctions to make living purposefully a highly probable situation. The following are a few belief systems to help you immensely along your path, even when the inevitable setbacks arrive.

1. MAKE THE CHOICE TO WIN even before you begin. Make it a CONVICTION.
2. Have the understanding and belief there are lessons in the setbacks. Regularly ask yourself "What can I learn from this?" and listen.
3. Adopt an attitude of happiness in general for your life. No matter what the conditions are, there is certainly someone in this world who is far less fortunate than you. Think about how many people cannot even read these words. You can.
4. Allow the lessons in the setbacks to help you make the minor tweaks and adjustments in your course so you can reach your outcome no matter the time frame.
5. Understand this journey is only for 90 days, three months out of the nine hundred and sixty expected months of your life! Yet these three months could COMPLETELY change the balance of your entire life.

Your internal belief system is your guide for these 90 days. I suggest you take a serious, honest "state of the union" within yourself and make the necessary adjustments before you begin and throughout the entire 90 days.

Smile. There are massive gifts in all of this!

What are you committed to living as YOUR PERSONAL MINDSET? What makes you feel empowered to believe? What makes you feel like nothing can stop you?

The Discipline Track

When it comes to being disciplined, most of us believe we can be very disciplined when in reality, we are not very good at it! Our minds have a terrible time being able to track how disciplined we are. Unless and until we have a specific way of logging what we do, we will always have distortion of the facts. Remember this, how you do one thing, is how you do everything. Being honest with your behaviors is definitely not an easy task. Some of us are too positive about our behaviors, claiming we get more done than we do. Even more of us, are far too negative about our behaviors, not claiming the wins we do have. Either way, creating discipline in our lives will benefit us.

Beginning today, start to track your progress. Make sure you download the log blocks from our website. Use those sheets to record your one simple task each day. Of course, if you do more than one simple task, record those as well. The rule, though, is to record one simple task per day. All of these one simple tasks add up over time and before you know it, you'll have 90 days completed and a minimum of 90 wins towards your goal. It's not glamorous, but it is effective!

Find someone in your immediate world, on your team, in your downline, anyone you feel compelled to work with that will hold you accountable, call you out when you don't show up and celebrate with you on a daily basis. In the event you would prefer not to discuss this 90 project with anyone, please know you are not alone. Honestly, I rarely share my 90 day outcomes with anyone, including my family. It has been my experience I do better if I make the commitment to myself, set myself up to win by organizing my immediate world around the outcome, then simply focusing on one task per day. There are many reasons why you may prefer to take this route; there is not a right way or a wrong way to cross the finish line. For me, I am very private with my outcomes, treating them as if they were treasured plants in my garden. If I nurture them intensely, giving them exactly what they need one on one, they will flourish. If I just talk about them without the nurturing one on one, they will die. Talking about your outcomes rarely helps them grow if the only point of the conversation is to let everyone know what you are doing!

Who is your accountability partner? Why did you choose this person?
What is their greatest strength in helping you achieve your outcome?

Even if you have chosen to have an accountability partner, make the commitment to
yourself to complete this outcome. Write out your commitment to yourself in detail.
I also HIGHLY RECOMMEND you copy this commitment you make to yourself and
HANG IT UP where you can see it every day. Remind yourself how much you care
about yourself and how committed you are to your longterm success.

Are You Ready To Be Brave?

In order to make it happen over the next 90 days, you will need a healthy dose of bravery. You must BELIEVE you can do this. You must BELIEVE you will do this. You must BELIEVE in your business. You must KNOW the next level in your life is on the other side of these 90 days.

Bravery is a choice. In order to be brave, you choose brave. Ask yourself "How can I be brave right now?" By asking the appropriate question, you align yourself with understanding bravery is a conscious choice.

Being brave doesn't mean not being scared. It means that you act in spite of the fear, knowing you will be frightened and that's OK! Even if you have never undertaken anything like this before, you will play full out and make changes in your life for the better.

Questions will arise. Feelings will show up. You will be tired. Time will fly by and you will wonder if you will make it to the end with your goal in hand. All the mind chatter will happen. Just keep moving forward. Keep doing what you have planned to do. Do one simple thing every day. Have fun in the process!

Most of all, be brave enough to begin! Starting is the hardest part. The first week is tough; the second is even harder. Breaking your own pattern of inactivity is challenging, but doable! You have already taken the first step by buying this book and reading it! Congratulations. Now it's time to be brave, plan your next 90 days and kick some ass.

Get a vision of bravery and make it clear as crystal in your heart and mind. I love to hang pictures of people I am in awe of, like Mother Teresa and Rosa Parks just to name a few; they make me realize what it's like to be an ordinary person and do extraordinary things.

Who inspires you? What is your vision of bravery?
Capture it now.

Letter from My Future Self

How do you think you will feel at the end of 90 days? What will you have accomplished? Who will you have become because you persevered? Let's take a few minutes and write today a letter to ourselves about what we expect at the end of 90 days.

It's Time To Begin Your New Story

I am assuming you have completed all of the exercises and are prepared to begin. The next 90 days will make a shift in your life if you play full out with the conviction of completion as well as the excitement of a child.

You are making a huge stride just by beginning the journey. Each day, with each step and each moment of focus on your outcome, you are one step closer to the desired result.

Nothing happens without the steps to make it happen. If you use the metaphor of building a house you will see exactly what I mean. You would not start off with an empty piece of land, hire a decorator, then take all the items you will use to decorate your rooms to the empty lot! There is a sequence to follow, very specific sequence: design, foundation, framing, inspections, electric, plumbing, sheet rock, fixtures, and paint. There are so many steps, most people hire an expert to take them through the process. A general contractor knows what should happen, when it should happen and how it should happen.
When you follow the plans, even though there may be set backs, you will end up with a beautiful place to live.

This is about YOU creating that beautiful place to live within yourself, as well as outside of yourself.

Follow the plan.
Stay focused on finishing.
Do the steps daily.
Most of all, SMILE while you are doing it.
This is your life.
Make it a masterpiece, one step at a time.

Commitment Contract

I, _____ , *am committed to showing up today and every day for the next 90 days, to do my absolute best! I will take consistent action every day for 90 days in order to create massive progress and reach my goal. I commit to completing the 90 days NO MATTER WHAT!! I will have fantastic days and days of struggle. I commit to noticing my patterns and improving my performance. I commit to myself to grow my business as I have designed for the next 90 days.*

Signature   *Date*

Let's Design Your 90 Plan!
The Action Path

1. Become CRYSTAL CLEAR on your specific outcome. Picture all the details because even the smallest of details will help compel you to make it happen. Make the picture of your outcome BIG and BRIGHT. Use your imagination. Include big, bold colors. Hear the applause. Embrace the deep sense of accomplishment.

2. Understand fully WHY you must have this outcome in your life. What will you gain by achieving this goal? What feelings will you experience when you reach the goal? How will it affect your life for the better? What are the consequences for yourself and your family if you don't achieve the goal? Your WHY must propel you to action.

3. What is your URGENCY??? What reason do you need to make this happen now?

4. What action items are necessary to make your outcome happen? This will be an ongoing list. It is the living "verb" part of your intention. Make a first pass at the list. Brain-dump everything you can think of in this moment—no matter how small. Don't allow your filters to come up telling you, "this will never work since it never has before." CAPTURE all the ideas you have to make your outcome a reality. Don't worry if you seem to have too few ideas. More ideas and steps will surface as you progress.

5. Evaluate your list of actions items to decide the order of importance. What will you do 1st, 2nd, 3rd, etc.?

6. Break out your action items into chunks of the 1st 30 days, the 2nd 30 days, and the final 30 days. Once again, don't be concerned if you seem to have everything in the first two groups. As you work through the plan and build on the action items you have completed, the next action items will organically come to you. Typically, you will be adding to the list weekly. Now you have established your master list.

7. Examine the action items and begin to transfer from the master list to your actual calendar for DAILY items to accomplish. This is a critical part of the process. Most items stay on someone's average "To Do List" and never make it to the calendar. If you don't assign it a day to be done, it won't get done! Visit our website, www.nailitin90.com, and download the 90-day log blocks to help you keep track of days and actions.

8. Schedule time each week to review your progress and adjust your strategy. Block out the time on your calendar right now. Half an hour sometime on Sunday normally sets you up for a productive week. Make sure you are reading the Daily Pages in this workbook. Decide on a time each day to answer the questions and write down your action items. Each weekly lesson and daily page will offer reminders of what you need to be doing.

9. If you are so inclined or consider yourself to be a very visual person, build a vision board of the outcome you are moving toward. Simply put, a vision board is a collage of pictures and words depicting your outcome as you desire it to be. I have been making vision boards for over two decades. I personally love to make mine large. I often take a picture of it to have on my phone or laptop. This is my personal treasure map. I hang it in my vanity area where I see it every time I brush my teeth. Put yours where you will see it daily. IN YOUR SIGHT! IN YOUR MIND! IN YOUR REALITY!

10. What is the absolute magic to all of this? MOMENT to MOMENT AWARENESS. Know what you are doing, how you are acting, and what is being projected. Step into the flow of your energy and own it.

IT IS IMPERATIVE YOU RECORD YOUR DAILY ACTION. REMEMBER, ONE SIMPLE ACTION TAKEN EVERYDAY WILL CHANGE YOUR BUSINESS! RECORDING YOUR ACTIONS GIVES YOU A PATH TO CELEBRATING YOUR WINS.

The Sample Action Path!

Let's consider the action path for promoting to the next level in your company's compensation plan. We will use one of my team members and the plan we created and she executed to secure a promotion in a little less than 90 days.

1. Become CRYSTAL CLEAR on your specific outcome. Picture all the details because even the smallest of details will help compel you to make it happen. Make the picture of your outcome BIG and BRIGHT. Use your imagination. Include big, bold colors. Hear the applause. Embrace the deep sense of accomplishment.

I am creating additional income for our family so my husband no longer has to put in so much over-time and work 70-80 hours a week. I can hear the laughter as our family has time to gather in the great room to play games. I see the sunshine warming us and the connections being made. My heart is overflowing because having close connection to family has always filled my cup.

2. Understand fully WHY you must have this outcome in your life. What will you gain by achieving this goal? What feelings will you experience when you reach the goal? How will it affect your life for

the better? What are the consequences for yourself and your family if you don't achieve the goal? Your WHY must propel you to action.

Promoting will build my confidence along with my income. Allowing my husband to work less will also improve all our family relationships. I am beginning to be a little scared and somewhat worried that all the hours he is working are taking a toll on his health. My why is to contribute to our family income and free up time for us all to be together.

3. What is your URGENCY??? What reason do you need to make this happen now?

My urgency has been created by three recent happenings. First, a good friend lost her husband unexpectedly at a young age. Second, an acquaintance took his own life because of the work pressures he was feeling to take care of his family. Lastly, I have watched several friends have their parents suffer from dementia or Alzheimers. Their spouse is still there to support them but they cannot even remember their name. My urgency is for us to be able to cherish each moment as a couple and a family and not take it for granted.

4. What are the action items are necessary to make your outcome happen? This will be an ongoing list. It is the living "verb" part of your

intention. Make a first pass at the list. Brain-dump everything you can think of in this moment—no matter how small. Don't allow your filters to come up telling you, "this will never work since it never has before." CAPTURE all the ideas you have to make your outcome a reality. Don't worry if you seem to have too few ideas. More ideas and steps will surface as you progress.

#14 Research groups to meet new people. Schedule time to attend groups.

#6 Review cell phone and social media contacts to create list of people I have never specifically asked about my business.

#9 Determine which live business presentations are close to me.

#5 Practice inviting people to look at my business.

#19 Research and review which welcome packet to use for training.

#17 Review all the online training videos so I will know what new team members are learning.

#15 Make a list of conference calls to inspire daily action.

#13 Learn about Power Hours and schedule into my week.

#7 Practice doing three-way calls on my phone to be sure I have it right.

#8 Ask 3-5 people to be available to do three-way calls with me.

#2 Know exactly how many people we need to add to the team to promote.

#3 Identify those active business builders on our team. Have a conversation with them about growing during the 90 days.

#12 Find a follow-up system being used in our business for all prospects so it can be scheduled.

#11 Have a 5-7 step plan for how to "drip" on potential team members.

#16 Go through all current and past customers to reach out.

#18 Be confident in teaching others to train their new team members.

#1 Share my commitment with my mentors along with my why.

#4 How many people must I talk to each week to bring in new team members?

#10 Invite prospects to look at my business.

5. Evaluate your list of actions items to decide the order of importance. What will you do 1st, 2nd, 3rd, etc.?

See the numbers indicated by each action item above

6. Break out your action items into chunks of the 1st 30 days, the 2nd 30 days, and the final 30 days. Once again, don't be concerned if you seem to have everything in the first two groups. As you work through the plan and build on the action items you have completed, the next action items will organically come to you.

Typically, you will be adding to the list weekly. Now you have established your master list.

FIRST 30 DAYS:

#1 Share my commitment with my mentors along with my why.

#2 Know exactly how many people we need to add to the team to promote.

#3 Identify those active business builders on our team. Have a conversation with them about growing during the 90 days.

#4 How many people must I talk to each week to bring in new team members?

#5 Practice inviting people to look at my business.

#6 Review cell phone and social media contacts to create list of people I have never specifically asked about my business.

#7 Practice doing three-way calls on my phone to be sure I have it right.

#8 Ask 3-5 people to be available to do three-way calls with me.

#9 Determine which live business presentations are close to me.

#10 Invite prospects to look at my business.

SECOND 30 DAYS:

#11 Have a 5-7 step plan for how to "drip" on potential team members.

#12 Find a follow-up system being used in our business for all prospects so it can be scheduled.

#13 Learn about Power Hours and schedule into my week.

#14 Research groups to meet new people. Schedule time to attend groups.

#15 Make a list of conference calls to inspire daily action.

#16 Go through all current and past customers to reach out.

THIRD 30 DAYS:

#17 Review all the online training videos so I will know what new team members are learning.

#18 Be confident in teaching others to train their new team members.

#19 Research and review which welcome packet to use for training.

7. Examine the action items and begin to transfer from the master list to your actual calendar for DAILY items to accomplish. This is a critical part of the process. Most items stay on someone's average "To Do List" and never make it to the calendar. If you don't assign it a day to be done, it won't get done! Visit our website, www.nailitin90.com, and download the 90-day log blocks to help you keep track of days and actions.

8. Schedule time each week to review your progress and adjust your strategy. Block out the time on your calendar right now. Half an hour sometime on Sunday normally sets you up for a productive

week. Make sure you are reading the Daily Pages in this workbook. Decide on a time each day to answer the questions and write down your action items. Each weekly lesson and daily page will offer reminders of what you need to be doing.

9. If you are so inclined or consider yourself to be a very visual person, build a vision board of the outcome you are moving toward. Simply put, a vision board is a collage of pictures and words depicting your outcome as you desire it to be. I have been making vision boards for over two decades. I personally love to make mine large. I often take a picture of it to have on my phone or laptop. This is my personal treasure map. I hang it in my vanity area where I see it every time I brush my teeth. Put yours where you will see it daily. IN YOUR SIGHT! IN YOUR MIND! IN YOUR REALITY!

10. What is the absolute magic to all of this? MOMENT to MOMENT AWARENESS. Know what you are doing, how you are acting, and what is being projected. Step into the flow of your energy and own it.

IT IS IMPERATIVE YOU RECORD YOUR DAILY ACTION. REMEMBER, ONE SIMPLE ACTION TAKEN EVERYDAY WILL CHANGE YOUR BUSINESS! RECORDING YOUR ACTIONS GIVES YOU A PATH TO CELEBRATING YOUR WINS.

Week One

Attitude & Mindset

Week One

Focus for the Week - Attitude & Mindset

When I was a child, I would often hear my father speak about the fact that attitude was everything. He would give me example after example of people who had challenges in their lives yet seem to overcome them simply with a great attitude. To be quite honest, this would irritate me. Because of my age I would only see the frustration and fully focus on that, not recognizing his point was to change my point of focus and thusly change my attitude.

Over the course of my life, I've come to realize while it's difficult to manage my attitude and mindset, I can do it and I'm much happier when I do do it. The question really comes down to HOW. I believe so many people become frustrated because they don't understand the HOW.

The simplest and quickest way to manage your mindset and your attitude is with questions. In all my years of coaching and strategy sessions with people, nothing, not one thing, has been as powerful as asking questions to shift perspective. Most people just ask very disempowering questions. Pause for a moment and ask yourself what kind of questions you ask internally throughout your day. It would be extremely beneficial to capture them and understand the power they have over you. Truth be told no two people are the same and that's why everyone has a different experience with every situation they encounter.

My favorite example is one my father used to use with me all the time. As his story goes, two children are starting school together for the first time and waiting for the bus. They both have the lunch boxes, new notebooks and new shoes. One of them looks very apprehensive while the other one is completely enthusiastic and can't wait to get there.
As the bus picks them up, the excited child springs onto the bus and grabs the seat behind the driver, while the other child sits towards the middle of the bus quietly. When the bus pulled up to school, all the children disembark with

different levels of enthusiasm; however, the enthusiastic child is wide-eyed with excitement. The other child is lagging behind looking down and not really chatting. Throughout the day, these two children continue to have very different experiences. The enthusiastic child is raising her hand at every chance while the apprehensive child keeps her head down and only engages when she has to. Both have their reasons for how they are showing up. It's a mix of how they were raised, what they think, and what they were told. Nonetheless, they are now in the same building, with the same teacher, in the same classroom, at the same chance for experience. At the end of the day, the bus takes the children home. Each child goes to their home and gives their parents an account of their day. That night, the two fathers have a conversation about the day. The father of the enthusiastic child is so excited about what his daughter told him, giving him all the juicy details of her wonderful day and how much she loved the teacher. The father of the apprehensive child is worried his child's not going to do well, telling the other father his daughter does not like the teacher and everything seems hard.

Can you see the difference between these two children, the two fathers and the experience? The very first thing you need to do is to look in your heart and see how you are "seeing" and "feeling" your experience. How you go into something matters! It's the fertile soil in which all successes born. How you control your attitude is the water in growing your success.

Capture your internal questions here. Keep the ones that work and give away the ones that don't. NO EXCUSES for keeping a poor question!

Week One

Day One

Theme – My attitude and mindset matter in every moment.

Quote – *Don't judge each day by the harvest you reap but by the seeds that you plant. - Robert Louis Stevenson*

Question – On your first day, what can you focus on to set the tone for your success for the entire week? Remember to think outside the box!

Action – Record your action for the day now!

Day Two

Theme – My attitude and mindset matter in every moment.

Quote – *People may hear your words, but they feel your attitude. -
John C. Maxwell*

Question – Who can you share you new attitude with today? How
will they know you are working on your attitude?

Action – Record your action for the day now!

Week One

Day Three

Theme – My attitude and mindset matter in every moment.

Quote – *Nothing can stop the man with the right mental attitude from achieving his goal; nothing on earth can help the man with the wrong mental attitude. - Thomas Jefferson*

Question – Check in each morning to make sure you start your day with the right mindset. What will your focus be? What direction is your mind taking today?

Action – Record your action for the day now!

Week One

Day Four

Theme – My attitude and mindset matter in every moment.

Quote – *Ability is what you're capable of doing. Motivation determines what you do. Attitude determines how well you do it.*
- Lou Holtz

Question – Are you focused on how much you enjoying your business? What do you need to do to enjoy it even more?

Action – Record your action for the day now!

Week One

Day Five

Theme – My attitude and mindset matter in every moment.

Quote – *Attitude is a little thing that makes a big difference.*
- Winston Churchill

Question – When things are not going as you plan, what will you do to manage your attitude in every moment?

Action – Record your action for the day now!

Week One

Day Six

Theme – My attitude and mindset matter in every moment.

Quote – *Watch your manner of speech if you wish to develop a peaceful state of mind. Start each day by affirming peaceful, contented and happy attitudes and your days will tend to be pleasant and successful. - Norman Vincent Peale*

Question – Everything you say to yourself matters. What are you habitually telling yourself? What are the questions that roam around your mind?

Action – Record your action for the day now!

Week One

Day Seven

Theme – My attitude and mindset matter in every moment.

Quote – *We cannot change our past. We can not change the fact that people act in a certain way. We can not change the inevitable. The only thing we can do is play on the one string we have, and that is our attitude. - Charles R. Swindoll*

Question – Who do you admire in business? Ask them on a walking date. Enjoy the time moving and asking great questions to learn from them.

Action – Record your action for the day now!

It's a Wrap! Week One

Congratulations! You completed your first week. Are you discovering how your small daily actions determine the overall trajectory of your life? You are on your way to creating the outcome you desire.

What do you feel great about from this first week?

What have you learned about yourself this week?

How will you adjust your daily actions for Week Two?

Review your Action Path now. Review the steps again. As you work through the steps, add new items as necessary. Take the time now to assign your actions to your calendar for Week Two.

Week Two

Clarity

Week Two

Focus for the Week - Clarity

Sometimes the biggest challenge we have is getting clear on what we want. While that seems crazy, it's actually quite common that we really don't know what we want. All too often when working with a client, I'll ask them "is that really what you want?" and they take a long pause, as if they're deep in thought. Again, all too often, the answer is "I'm actually not sure." This happens over and over and over again. One would think if it is our goal, then we should be clear on what the goal is. Wrong! Getting clearer is probably the most difficult task I do with new coaching clients. Often we confuse old goals with new goals, wants, desires, needs: it becomes one giant jumbled mess with a seemingly endless variety of options.

Let's save a bunch of time and aggravation, right here and right now. Check in with your goals. Make sure as we go into week two, they are still in line with what you want or believed you wanted when we started this program. If not, no worries! Let's make the adjustment now and move forward. There is nothing to be ashamed of in shifting goals and outcomes. The tragedy comes when we wait too long and continue down a road that makes us unhappy and unfulfilled. Now is the time to do to your soul-searching.

Am I still aligned with my original outcome?

Week Two

Day Eight

Theme – My clarity is what keeps me on track.

Quote – *The greatest beauty always lies in the greatest clarity.*
- Gotthold Ephraim Lessing

Question – As we tune our clarity, life changes. What are you clear on today? What can you see better than ever now?

Action – Record your action for the day now!

Week Two

Day Nine

Theme – My clarity is what keeps me on track.

Quote – *The beauty is that through disappointment you can gain clarity, and with clarity comes conviction and true originality.*
-Conan O'Brien

Question – Disappointment happens. How you transform it matters. How will you transform any disappointment today?

Action – Record your action for the day now!

Week Two

Day Ten

Theme – My clarity is what keeps me on track.

Quote – *Mindfulness is about love and loving life. When you cultivate this love, it gives you clarity and compassion for life, and your actions happen in accordance with that. -Jon Kabat-Zinn*

Question – How mindful are you being in your life? What clarity have you discovered today?

Action – Record your action for the day now!

Week Two

Day Eleven

Theme – My clarity is what keeps me on track.

Quote – *Children are remarkable for their intelligence and ardor, for their curiosity, their intolerance of shams, the clarity and ruthlessness of their vision. -Aldous Huxley*

Question – Children have the ability to live with supreme clarity about what they want. What do you really want? How clearly do you see it?

Action – Record your action for the day now!

Week Two

Day Twelve

Theme – My clarity is what keeps me on track.

Quote – *At some point, a flash of sustained clarity reveals the difference between what someone would have you believe is true, and what you know from the depths of your own heart to the peaks of your soul to be true. What happens after that is up to you.*
-Aberjhani

Question – In each decision, your life is shaped. What do you have that is shaping your life today?

Action – Record your action for the day now!

Week Two

Day Thirteen

Theme – My clarity is what keeps me on track.

Quote – *People are remarkably bad at remembering long lists of goals. I learned this at a professional level when trying to get my high-performance coaching clients to stay on track; the longer their lists of to-dos and goals, the more overwhelmed and off-track they got. Clarity comes with simplicity. -Brendon Burchard*

Question – What can you simplify today?

Action – Record your action for the day now!

Week Two

Day Fourteen

Theme – My clarity is what keeps me on track.

Quote – *For me, an area of moral clarity is: you're in front of someone who's suffering and you have the tools at your disposal to alleviate that suffering or even eradicate it, and you act. - Paul Farmer*

Question – Who can you help today? Who can benefit from what you know or what you do?

Action – Record your action for the day now!

It's a Wrap! Week Two

Fourteen days. Fourteen completed action items. Celebrate how far you have come! Are you creating better habits? Do you feel a sense of accomplishment each day when you action items are complete?

What do you feel great about so far in the process?

What have you learned about yourself this week?

How will you adjust your daily actions for Week Three?

Review your Action Path now. Review the steps again. As you work through the steps, add new items as necessary. Take the time now to assign your actions for Week Three.

Week Three

Connection - The Seen

Week Three

Focus for the Week - Connection - The Seen

All too often we miss what is right under our nose. One thing I appreciate greatly about network marketing is the fact they ask you to talk to people you know, letting everyone know what you're doing. For some people, this may seem absolutely overwhelming. However, I would like to offer you a different point of view.

We spend so much time in our lives ignoring what's within our reach. We are overwhelmed and drowning in a world of details and overstimulation. To cope with this, our brains have become deletion creatures. One of the biggest byproducts of this, sadly, is we no longer reach out in genuine connection with others. A quick text message here and there, a post on Facebook, maybe an e-mail and we're on our way. While this is fine, quite often it leaves us feeling empty. Then all of a sudden we're in a business that requires us to connect with people. The kind of connection with genuine feeling, the one that influences people to actually purchase from us. But wait, we haven't talked to these people one-on-one in a very, very, long time. So we start making these calls and we start reaching out. It feels awkward and inauthentic, maybe even desperate. They don't react the way we want. We don't feel the way we should and all of a sudden we're wondering why we got into this business.

The cure? The cure is the same cure humanity needs as well; genuine heartfelt connection. People want to be seen; they want to know they matter. In general, most people feel neglected. I hear this day after day in my coaching sessions. Wives wonder why their husbands don't notice all they do. Husbands wonder why their wives don't appreciate all they do. Very few feel heard when they speak. Our children spend less and less time with us and more and more time with teachers and after school activities. All of this only adds to the feeling of overwhelm people experience. This is shocking since the need for connection is the highest driving force most people have. The crazy part of all of this, most of us don't even recognize this is what's happening. We think we need to look for a new job, or a new place to live, or a new spouse, never truly realizing all we need to do is pause and take a moment and connect with somebody. We thoughtfully titled this week about Connection - The Seen. Pause for a moment and think about how many people you actually "see" in your day. Of course, you walk past people all day long, but do you really even notice them? How many people do you smile at as you pass by? How many people do you make eye contact with? How many people do you make small talk with and actually listen to what they're saying?

These small distinctions can make a huge difference not only in your business but in the lives of the people you actually touch. It has been my experience that when we offer ourselves up for connection, people will reach out and take it. The reality, most people are thrilled. They are experiencing the same deprivation of connection you yourself probably feel. I often tell my children to smile at people because you may be the only person that smiled at them today. My seven-year-old seemed shocked by this, looking at me like I was crazy. You see in his world, he smiles at everyone he talks to. He is still in his raw, child state of being. My husband and I work very hard to make sure he stays a child as long as he can. He has plenty of play time, not being overcommitted. He's surrounded by old-school toys that make him think and use his imagination. Electronics are extremely limited. Allowing his creativity to flow is our priority. All of this is designed to keep him connected to himself and allow him with connect to others.

If you are experiencing a moment, as you read this, where all of a sudden you're questioning how connected you are, then I suggest you pause, and do for yourself what we do for ourselves and our son. Take a day or two, and do nothing but focus on your creativity, your imagination, your connection and yourself. Allow yourself the gift first to connect with yourself and then go out and smile at people. If you can build this skill back up to the point it was when you were a child, you will be amazed at how your business grows. The simple fact that you are no longer selling to people and you are connecting with people will change you and your business.

This week, make your focus the people you know. Give them the gift of giving your full attention to them. Allow yourself to feel the gift of being completely present, in the moment.

Week Three

Day Fifteen

Theme – Connection is available anytime and is all around me.

Quote – *When the trainer talks to the fighter, there's a connection.*
You don't always have to say much. -Sugar Ray Leonard

Question – How well are you connecting without using words?
Practice finding ways to connect without words.

Action – Record your action for the day now!

Week Three

Day Sixteen

Theme – Connection is available anytime and is all around me.

Quote – *Many believe effective networking is done face-to-face, building a rapport with someone by looking at them in the eye, leading to a solid connection and foundational trust.*
- Raymond Arroyo

Question – When you have the chance to be with others, how well are you connecting with them? Are you 100% with them or is your mind somewhere else?

Action – Record your action for the day now!

Week Three

Day Seventeen

Theme – Connection is available anytime and is all around me.

Quote – *Since you cannot do good to all, you are to pay special attention to those who, by the accidents of time, or place, or circumstances, are brought into closer connection with you. - Saint Augustine*

Question – If someone comes to you, there is a reason. How can you make them feel special and connect with them?

Action – Record your action for the day now!

Week Three

Day Eighteen

Theme – Connection is available anytime and is all around me.

Quote – *Vulnerability is the birthplace of connection and the path to the feeling of worthiness. If it doesn't feel vulnerable, the sharing is probably not constructive. - Brene Brown*

Question – How can you be vulnerable with someone today? How can you share a piece of yourself, allowing them to share the real you?

Action – Record your action for the day now!

Week Three

Day Nineteen

Theme – Connection is available anytime and is all around me.

Quote – *I feel like the reason people feel like they know me is because I'm giving you myself in the music. There's where the connection comes from; you can't Twitter that. - J. Cole*

Question – When you are present, you connect. How can you make yourself even more present and connected today?

Action – Record your action for the day now!

Week Three

Day Twenty

Theme – Connection is available anytime and is all around me.

Quote – *Until I realized that rock music was my connection to the rest of the human race, I felt like I was dying, for some reason, and I didn't know why.- Bruce Springsteen*

Question – When we don't connect, we are dying inside. Find someone and connect to what's important today.

Action – Record your action for the day now!

Week Three

Day Twenty-One

Theme – Connection is available anytime and is all around me.

Quote – *I think there's some connection between absolute discipline and absolute freedom. - Alan Rickman*

Question – As we enter into day 21, what have you become disciplined with and are starting to feel freedom with?

Action – Record your action for the day now!

It's a Wrap! Week Three

Three weeks of focused effort toward your outcome. Wow! Take a deep breath. Reflect on the momentum you are building.

What are some of your "wins" this week?

What emotions have surfaced for you in these three weeks?

How will you adjust your daily actions for Week Four?

Review your Action Path now. Review the steps again. As you work through the steps, add new items as necessary. Take the time now to assign your actions for Week Four.

Week Four

Consistency Of Who You Are

Week Four

Focus for the Week - Consistency Of Who You Are

In the world of network marketing, we know consistency wins the game. But what specifically should you be consistent with? Your connections? Your downline? Your up-line? WHAT? The feeling of trying to keep track of it all can swallow you up as we have pointed out earlier. The best way to combat this feeling is to create rituals that support the business you envision and stick to them. Please notice I did not say habits. I believe habits are not as coveted as rituals. Think about how much better you feel if you say you have a ritual instead of a habit. The word habit is mostly used when we are talking about breaking out of something, whereas a ritual sounds like we have chosen the tasks with much thought and precision.

All of this boils down to remaining consistent with the new version of yourself and the empowering rituals you have created. Please understand I am very aware this task is probably the most challenging of all the tasks we ask you to do in the entire book. Humans, in general, have an extremely hard time remaining consistent with their behaviors. Mostly because we are great at telling ourselves stories in order to keep it all together! We seem to have an uncanny ability to deny the obvious when it comes to ourselves, what our true habits are daily. And let's not forget, all too often we will say we will start tomorrow. To me, this is the killer of dreams: tomorrow.

If we are constantly waiting for tomorrow to arrive, we never have the moment to start. Consistency begins in this moment, not tomorrow. Of course, there will be ups and downs. Of course, you will be challenged to stick to a consistent ritual, but that does not mean you give up and say I'll just start again tomorrow. That habit in itself robs you of any wins in the day. Every moment is available to begin, and every moment is a new chance to be consistent. Seize the moment. Consistency begins now, and consistency with your business first begins with who you are.

What are you waiting for?

Week Four

Day Twenty-Two

Theme – I am consistent in who I am and how I show up everyday.

Quote – *One isn't necessarily born with courage, but one is born with potential. Without courage, we cannot practice any other virtue with consistency. We can't be kind, true, merciful, generous, or honest.*
- Maya Angelou

Question – As you enter into week four, what have you become disciplined with and are starting to feel freedom with?

Action – Record your action for the day now!

Week Four

Day Twenty-Three

Theme – I am consistent in who I am and how I show up everyday.

Quote – *Trust is built with consistency. - Lincoln Chafee*

Question – What needs to become a ritual in your business? Your life? What are you letting slip through the cracks?

Action – Record your action for the day now!

Week Four

Day Twenty-Four

Theme – I am consistent in who I am and how I show up everyday.

Quote – *In baseball, my theory is to strive for consistency, not to worry about the numbers. If you dwell on statistics you get shortsighted, if you aim for consistency, the numbers will be there at the end. - Tom Seaver*

Question – What are you focusing on today? What is going well or what is challenging you? Tune it to how you are showing up.

Action – Record your action for the day now!

Week Four

Day Twenty-Five

Theme – I am consistent in who I am and how I show up everyday.

Quote – *Leadership can't be fabricated. If it is fabricated and rehearsed, you can't fool the guys in the locker room. So when you talk about leadership, it comes with performance. Leadership comes with consistency. - Junior Seau*

Question – Are you showing your team how consistent you are? Are you an example for them?

Action – Record your action for the day now!

Week Four

Day Twenty-Six

Theme – I am consistent in who I am and how I show up everyday.

Quote – *People like consistency. Whether it's a store or a restaurant, they want to come in and see what you are famous for.*
- Millard Drexler

Question – Is your consistent behavior serving you or hurting you? Are you creating rituals or serving habits?

Action – Record your action for the day now!

Week Four

Day Twenty-Seven

Theme – I am consistent in who I am and how I show up everyday.

Quote – *For me, integrity is the consistency of words and actions. Part of the way that you do that is to ask people questions on some of the most difficult issues that you confront. 'Take me through where you felt you had to compromise your values.' - Kenneth Chenault*

Question – Are your words matching your actions? Are your actions serving your life and your business?

Action – Record your action for the day now!

Week Four

Day Twenty-Eight

Theme – I am consistent in who I am and how I show up everyday.

Quote – *When you look at people who are successful, you will find that they aren't the people who are motivated, but have consistency in their motivation. - Arsene Wegner*

Question – On the last day of week four, what is your greatest take-away?

Action – Record your action for the day now!

It's a Wrap! Week Four

Give yourself a pat on the back! You are two short days from completing your first thirty days of action!

What feelings showed up for you this week?

What made you feel a sense of accomplishment?

How will you adjust your daily actions for Week Five?

Review your Action Path now. Review the steps again. As you work through the steps, add new items as necessary. Take the time now to assign your actions for Week Five.

Week Five

Self-Leadership - Managing Your Time & Energy

Week Five

Focus for the Week - Self Leadership

The definition of leadership is "the action of leading a group of people or an organization" indicating there is a leader and a follower. So what does Self-Leadership mean? When you are in a position of having to make a decision, contemplating all of the options, you come to a place where it's time to decide. The next step is your choice, no matter what the outcome is. Having an awareness of making the decision and knowing you must make the decision for yourself, to me, is the definition of self-leadership.

Being able to contemplate the consequences of your choices deepens your level of self-leadership. When you can think forward, discerning the outcome before it happens, or, at least, the possible outcome before it happens, in that time and space you are leading yourself. Self-leadership is being able to do the things you know you need to do while still not wanting to do them. Holding yourself to the standards you set for yourself, without compromising the beliefs you love and hold dear, you are a leader. When you lead yourself first, others want to follow you. They see you doing what they wish they could and choose you to lead them.

This all begins with Self-leadership. If your dream is to build a team of people that are empowered, you must first empower yourself. As you progress through this week, think about all the opportunities it will afford you to test yourself, to truly lead yourself. Make no mistake about it, this is a moment to moment opportunity. Whether or not you should eat the ice cream, whether or not you should spend the money, whether or not you should go to the gym, each one of those is a moment for self-leadership.

If you knew your team was watching, how would you show up?

Week Five

Day Twenty-Nine

Theme – I MUST lead myself first and foremost with love & intention.

Quote – *If your actions inspire others to dream more, learn more, do more and become more, you are a leader. - John Quincy Adams*

Question – Are you being the best example you can be for yourself so your light shines the way for your team?

Action – Record your action for the day now!

Week Five

Day Thirty

Theme – I MUST lead myself first and foremost with love & intention.

Quote – *If the highest aim of a captain were to preserve his ship, he would keep it in port forever.- Thomas Aquinas*

Question – What is the highest aim you have for yourself within your heart this week?

Action – Record your action for the day now!

Week Five

Day Thirty-One

Theme – I MUST lead myself first and foremost with love & intention.

Quote – *Good management is the art of making problems so interesting and their solutions so constructive that everyone wants to get to work and deal with them. - Paul Hawken*

Question – What challenge can you see as "interesting" today? What is the "constructive" solution you can use to tackle the challenge?

Action – Record your action for the day now!

Week Five

Day Thirty-Two

Theme – I MUST lead myself first and foremost with love & intention.

Quote – *Example is leadership. - Albert Schweitzer*

Question – You are the best example of what you believe. What are you showing the world today about yourself?

Action – Record your action for the day now!

Week Five

Day Thirty-Three

Theme – I MUST lead myself first and foremost with love & intention.

Quote – *Go as far as you can see; when you get there, you'll be able to see farther. - J. P. Morgan*

Question – Are you giving yourself grief for where you are in your journey? Are you being too hard on yourself?

Action – Record your action for the day now!

Week Five

Day Thirty-Four

Theme – I MUST lead myself first and foremost with love & intention.

Quote – *If you want a quality, act as if you already had it.*
- William James

Question – What part of your self-leadership do you "act as if" till you arrive?

Action – Record your action for the day now!

Week Five

Day Thirty-Five

Theme – I MUST lead myself first and foremost with love & intention.

Quote – *I look for what needs to be done. After all, that's how the universe designs itself. - R. Buckminster Fuller*

Question – What really needs to be taken care of for me to lead in love & intention?

Action – Record your action for the day now!

It's a Wrap! Week Five

Evaluate and celebrate how far you have come! You have accumulated thirty-five action steps toward your goal.

What do you feel great about this week?

How has your attitude towards your business changed?

How will you adjust your daily actions for Week Six?

Review your Action Path now. Review the steps again. As you work through the steps, add new items as necessary. Take the time now to assign your actions for Week Six.

Week Six

Connection - The UNSEEN

Week Six

Focus for the Week - Connection - The Unseen

Exactly how do you connect with people you don't know and technically can't see? I'm referring to the people that come to you without referrals. People may respond to a post on Facebook, a postcard you've left somewhere, or a video you've posted. Technically, the only way this person has a connection to you is through the connection they make in their own mind when they see you on a video or they read your Facebook post. Their evaluation of how engaged they are with you in the moment determines their evaluation of what you said and rates its value. Their imagination connects the dots.

The way to be successful in connecting with the Unseen is to put yourself in the position they would be in and pretend you're them. Start to think about what that person would be looking for, and then you write what you would want to find, record what you would want to hear. As I have stated earlier, everyone wants to know they are seen. The trick here is allowing someone to feel seen when you have yet to see them physically. Building that connection and allowing them to feel you have a commonality immediately is what needs to happen. So why am I getting so specific about this? Because when most sellers put together the messaging for the people who will find the postcards or the video or the post, they start to speak very technically and start acting very stiff. It feels very robotic. How that translates to the person on the other side - disconnection. The very thing you are trying to avoid you are achieving!

This week as you enter week six, make it a point to put things out you would want to read, would get your attention and make you feel as though you were talking to a genuinely wonderful human being. Write from your heart, speak from your heart. Let someone feel loved even though they have never seen you in person.

Week Six

Day Thirty-Six

Theme – Connection happens in many forms, even if you can't see it.

Quote – *Everybody laughs the same in every language because laughter is a universal connection. - Yakov Smirnoff*

Question – How can you make someone feel your enthusiasm for life today? What would it be like to provide a random surprise for an unknown person?

Action – Record your action for the day now!

Week Six

Day Thirty-Seven

Theme – Connection happens in many forms, even if you can't see it.

Quote – *Every living being is an engine geared to the wheel-work of the universe. Though seemingly affected only by its immediate surrounding, the sphere of external influence extends to infinite distance. - Nikola Tesla*

Question – You are so much more than you know. Who in the world could benefit from discovering something from you today?

Action – Record your action for the day now!

Week Six

Day Thirty-Eight

Theme – Connection happens in many forms, even if you can't see it.

Quote – *Life is like a landscape. You live in the midst of it but can describe it only from the vantage point of distance.*
- Charles Lindbergh

Question – Today, are you paying attention to the world around you or are you not taking it all in?

Action – Record your action for the day now!

Week Six

Day Thirty-Nine

Theme – Connection happens in many forms, even if you can't see it.

Quote – *Laughter gives us distance. It allows us to step back from an event, deal with it and then move on. - Bob Newhart*

Question – What can you heal with laughter today?

Action – Record your action for the day now!

Week Six

Day Forty

Theme – Connection happens in many forms, even if you can't see it.

Quote – *We humans are hard to deal with. We are a loud, complex and demanding bunch. - Henry Rollins*

Question – Sometimes distance makes it easier to connect. Who can you connect with today that may have challenged you previously?

Action – Record your action for the day now!

Week Six

Day Forty-One

Theme – Connection happens in many forms, even if you can't see it.

Quote – *No distance of place or lapse of time can lessen the friendship of those who are thoroughly persuaded of each other's worth. - Robert Southey*

Question – Rapport is possible from anywhere, distance or close. Who are you building rapport with here today?

Action – Record your action for the day now!

Week Six

Day Forty-Two

Theme – Connection happens in many forms, even if you can't see it.

Quote – *I always think it's interesting to dig a little bit deeper every time you go to someplace that seems like a revelation or a strong connection to an emotional truth. - Carly Simon*

Question – As we enter day 42, how can you connect with someone on a deeper level and let them know you care?

Action – Record your action for the day now!

It's a Wrap! Week Six

As you approach the halfway point in this 90 day journey, take a moment to congratulate yourself on your consistent, persistent efforts. Smile.

How has your mindset shifted?

What leadership traits are emerging in you?

How will you adjust your daily actions for Week Seven?

Review your Action Path now. Review the steps again. As you work through the steps, add new items as necessary. Take the time now to assign your actions for Week Seven.

Week Seven

Self-Care

Week Seven

Focus for the Week - Self-Care

As you approach the halfway mark in this 90 day journey, how are you feeling physically and emotionally? You are making significant progress toward your desired outcome. Are you properly taking care of yourself along the way? It is imperative to success for you to be healthy and happy enough to enjoy the success you create.

Self-care means making sure your body and your mind are in the proper place to enjoy the outcomes you are creating and to carry on jubilantly to the next step in your success journey.

Physically one of the most important things you can do is drink water. Do you fill yourself with coffee and soda? They are not nourishing you. Your body needs water for all of its basic functions. If you are having trouble focusing or you are tripping over your words, drink water. The rule is you should drink half your body weight in ounces of water each day. So if you weigh 135 pounds, you will consume 68 ounces or about 8 ½ glasses of water each day. Measure it out in the morning and drink all day.

We all know nutritious food feeds our body. Avoid the drive-thru and fast food. Lean towards fruits, veggies and lean protein. Be prepared. If you are out and about often, keep a case of water in the trunk or back seat of your car. Have snacks in your purse, briefcase or console. Protein bars, almonds, apples, boiled eggs. We all know how to properly feed our bodies. Let's be prepared so it is simple.

Quiet time is another form of self-care. When you arise each morning, take a few minutes to pray or meditate. Take a quiet walk and enjoy nature. You want to refill your tank on a daily basis. Allow yourself 10-30 minutes alone to get centered. If you don't take time to replenish your own energy, you won't be able to give to others at the highest level.

Reward yourself! You work hard, so it is important to play hard. Maybe you need a night away in a fancy hotel with your sweetheart. Could it just be a break for a mani/pedi will raise your spirits and give you a much needed hour break? Maybe it is time for a full body massage or to stop in for a little reflexology at the foot spa.

Socialize while you exercise. Invite someone you would normally have coffee with to take a walk with you. Get on the tennis courts or the golf course. Take a bike ride around the lake. Movement creates energy.

Do you love the beach? The mountains? Listening to the rainfall? Make time for moments that fill your soul. What good is financial success if you aren't embracing and creating magic moments along the way?

Take time for yourself! Self-care allows you to be your optimal self so you can serve others and build a thriving business.

You have brains in your head.
You have feet in your shoes.
You can steer yourself any direction you choose.
-Dr. Seuss, *Oh, The Places You'll Go!*

Week Seven

Day Forty-Three

Theme – I deserve happiness and success every day.

Quote – *No matter how much you know, there is always someone you can learn from that knows more. - Steve Thompson, Relationship Marketing*

Question – Who do you admire in business? Ask them on a walking date. Enjoy the time moving and asking great questions to learn from them.

Action – Record your action for the day now!

Week Seven

Day Forty-Four

Theme – I deserve happiness and success every day.

Quote – *Work harder on yourself than you do your job. If you work hard on your job you can make a living. If you work hard on yourself, you can make a fortune.* –*Jim Rohn*

Question – How much water did you drink yesterday? Step it up a notch. How much will you measure out to drink today?

Action – Record your action for the day now!

Week Seven

Day Forty-Five

Theme – I deserve happiness and success every day.

Quote – *Develop and nurture a positive mindset and create a daily habit of focusing only on what is going right. You will get more of what you focus your attention on…celebrate all your successes, even the small ones, so you feel good. -Monica Ramos, Behind Her Brand: Direct Sales Edition*

Question – How can you create quiet time to nourish your soul? Will you read a devotional? Meditate? Listen to an inspirational book? Make a plan.

Action – Record your action for the day now!

Week Seven

Day Forty-Six

Theme – I deserve happiness and success every day.

Quote – *At the end of the day, we will look back with either satisfaction or regret. Make a decision to live a satisfying life now.*
- Susan Sly

Question – How will you reward yourself today? You are half way through the 90 day journey. Give yourself an ovation and a reward.

Action – Record your action for the day now!

Week Seven

Day Forty-Seven

Theme – I deserve happiness and success every day.

Quote – *Most of the overnight success you've heard about, there's five to ten years of invisible, you never saw, hard work that went into that success. -Eric Worre, Network Marketing Pro*

Question – How will you incorporate exercise into your day?

Action – Record your action for the day now!

Week Seven

Day Forty-Eight

Theme – I deserve happiness and success every day.

Quote – *The goal is not to get rich. The goal is to live rich. -Darren Hardy, Publisher, Success Magazine*

Question – How will you prepare to improve your nutrition today? Prepare healthy snacks? Plan tomorrow's meals today?

Action – Record your action for the day now!

Week Seven

Day Forty-Nine

Theme – I deserve happiness and success every day.

Quote – *Your greatest gift to others is being yourself, and what a rare gift that is. It is in being yourself that you have absolutely no competition. -Tammy Stanley, Carpe Phonum*

Question – What do you consider a decadent pleasure? Maybe today is the day to splurge!

Action – Record your action for the day now!

It's a Wrap! Week Seven

Tomorrow is Day 50! Your progress is substantial. Focus on your outcome today. See the progress you have made because you decided you must.

What thoughts come up for you about yourself today?

How will you reward yourself for completing 50 days of action items?

How will you adjust your daily actions for Week Eight?

Review your Action Path now. Review the steps again. As you work through the steps, add new items as necessary. Take the time now to assign your actions for Week Eight.

Week Eight

Connection with Groups

Week Eight

Focus for the Week - Connection with Groups

It has been said people are more afraid of public speaking than they are of dying. If you feel this way, it is time to look at speaking to groups in a whole new light. To succeed at a high level in direct selling, you must be willing to present to groups and be vulnerable. No one is ever perfect. In our industry not being perfect is really good news.

Remember, from the first minute you approach a prospect, you are demonstrating to them what they will be doing if they join your business. Therefore, keep it simple. Be polished and professional. Do not strive for perfect.

A group is just a collection or cluster of people. You are presenting your ideas to a group when you share about the book you just read with three of your friends over coffee. In that instance, you are likely very relaxed because you know the people and have an idea of their reactions to your thoughts and input.

Speaking to groups to build your business comes in two forms. First, when you speak with two or more people specifically showing them your product or your opportunity. Most network marketers are passionate about their products which makes sharing them easy. Just talk about what you love. When it comes to sharing about the opportunity, we all of a sudden get a bit antsy. What causes this? Belief. You must choose to be as passionate and believe in your opportunity as deeply as you do the product. When you make this shift in your belief about the opportunity, your passion will come through when you present how others can join your business.

The other type of speaking to groups is finding gatherings where you can add value with information. Share important skills with others they can develop to improve their business. In this case, you do not talk about your specific product or your company, instead present ideas around your product to help the audience. They will be drawn to your excitement and appreciate how you have added value to them. For example, if you are in the electricity and natural gas business, you can do presentations at networking groups, rotary clubs, chamber events, etc. Make your presentation about how to make a home more energy efficient. Give away a small item at the end which helps improve energy efficiency like the foam inserts used in wall plugs to keep air from seeping in or out of the house.

If you are in the jewelry, makeup or clothing business, do presentations to women's groups, moms of multiples or career women's groups. Make it about image. Share what you know about coloring or choosing the way clothes fit your body. You get the idea. You can create a short presentation to offer great value to the audience around candles, supplements, weight loss, water, essential oils, etc. You don't have to talk about your business to offer insights to a large group.

The audience wants to feel connected to you. Whether it is two people or forty people, make sure you consciously connect with each person. Here are several ideas for group connection:

- If you are speaking to a larger group, arrive early and introduce yourself to several audience members in advance. Now you have friends in the audience. You may even be able to refer to them by name during your presentation.

- Allow yourself to really be with one person at a time while you are speaking. In other words, connect eye to eye with audience members for a few seconds before moving to the next person.

- Remember to breathe while you speak.

- Keep your body language open and friendly. Shoulders back. Smile on face. Confident and centered.

- In a smaller group, ask each person individually if they have questions. Look them in the eye. Listen attentively and then answer authentically. If you don't know the answer to their question, that is fine. Commit to finding out the answer and getting back to them in a timely manner.

Consider how fun it will be to speak to groups and make connections to build your business for the long-term. Take a moment to brainstorm a few groups who might be interested in having you do a brief presentation.

You may not ever be a keynote speaker electrifying audiences of thousands with your stories and presence. What you will be is an influential presenter who connects with the audience compelling them to want to do business with you.

Week Eight

Day Fifty

Theme – My positive energy impacts each group I encounter.

Quote – *When you focus on money, the people don't come. When you focus on people, that is when the money comes.*
–Todd Falcone, The Fearless Networker

Question – What feelings arise when you think about presenting to a group? Do these feelings support you or undermine you?

Action – Record your action for the day now!

Week Eight

Day Fifty-One

Theme – My positive energy impacts each group I encounter.

Quote – *To live your greatest life, you must first become a leader within yourself. Take charge of your life. Begin attracting and manifesting all that you desire in life. -Sonia Ricotti*

Question – When will you gather a small group to present your product or opportunity? Will you set a regular schedule?

Action – Record your action for the day now!

Week Eight

Day Fifty-Two

Theme – My positive energy impacts each group I encounter.

Quote – *Sometimes all you need is twenty seconds of insane courage and I promise you something great will come of it. - From the motion picture 'We Bought A Zoo'*

Question – How will improving confidence in my presentation abilities effect my business?

Action – Record your action for the day now!

Week Eight

Day Fifty-Three

Theme – My positive energy impacts each group I encounter.

Quote – *Do the difficult things while they are easy and do the great things while they are small. A journey of a thousand miles must begin with a single step. -Lao Tzu*

Question – How will I practice my presentation skills this week? Speak up at book club or Bible study?

Action – Record your action for the day now!

Week Eight

Day Fifty-Four

Theme – My positive energy impacts each group I encounter.

Quote – *Be alert to opportunities but always seek to serve, not sell. If you truly focus on helping others, they will help you. -Steve Thompson, Relationship Marketing*

Question – What are three points I could present in a brief value-filled message related to my product or service?

Action – Record your action for the day now!

Week Eight

Day Fifty-Five

Theme – My positive energy impacts each group I encounter.

Quote – *There is no passion to be found playing small – in settling for a life that is less than the one you are capable of living.*
-Nelson Mandela

Question – Who will I share the idea of presenting a value-filled message with so they can help with group ideas?

Action – Record your action for the day now!

Week Eight

Day Fifty-Six

Theme – My positive energy impacts each group I encounter.

Quote – *Prosperity doesn't happen for the lucky. It is created by self-discipline, work, guts, and providing value to others. -Randy Gage*

Question – What will I do today to improve my presentation skills?

Action – Record your action for the day now!

It's a Wrap! Week Eight

How committed are you to your outcome? Have you adjusted or shifted your belief in yourself to a higher level?

How are you handling disappointments when they show up?

How are you re-focusing your mindset on difficult days?

How will you adjust your daily actions for Week Nine?

Review your Action Path now. Review the steps again. As you work through the steps, add new items as necessary. Take the time now to assign your actions for Week Nine.

Week Nine

Mapping Your Success

Week Nine

Focus for the Week - Mapping Your Success

How are your results in proportion to your activity? Measuring your activity versus your productivity will offer the insight you need to improve. You may need to alter the activities you are performing to increase your results.

If you do not measure your activity, how do you know what is and is not creating results. With my team we use Activity Tracking sheets and Power Hour sheets. Every day of every week, we track how many calls we make, messages we leave, conversations we have, presentations we make for products and opportunity, all on our Activity Tracking sheets. We track the number of "no" responses along with new customers and team members. When someone is struggling, we can look at the activity and make a new course of action to help them succeed. When someone is having massive success, we can pinpoint the activity working the best for them and focus on doing more of that activity. Activity creates productivity.

Let's be clear. Activity means income-producing activities. It does not mean wasting time on social media or sending mass emails. We have firmly established when discussing networking, your goal must be to build relationships. People want to do business with those they like. How can they like you if they don't know you? A large part of activity is relationship building.

What about Power Hour sheets? Another way to plan and measure is to create time during your week to have Power Hours. Making calls. On my sheets, I list people I want to invite to see my product or my business as well as touching base with team members. I write names on the list during the week and when I have a Power Hour scheduled, I already know who I am going to call and the purpose of each call.

Do you track your daily mode of operation? Often referred to as your DMO.
If you are building your business part-time, maybe your DMO is 1 and 1.
Reach out to one new prospect each day and follow up with a prospect each
day. If you have more time, your DMO may build on this to include at least
one presentation a day. If your team is growing or larger, your DMO may
include talking to those on your team who are close to promoting to the next
level in your company. Make a checklist for your DMO. Don't make the list
so long you feel overwhelmed and can never complete the daily activities.
Set yourself up for success. Make your DMO checklist with income-
producing activities. Do them every day and your business will grow.

Focused activity leads to productivity which leads to increased income.

Week Nine

Day Fifty-Seven

Theme – I measure my progress step by step.

Quote – *Don't compare your beginning to someone else's middle.*
–Jon Acuff

Question – What daily activities are vital in my business?

Action – Record your action for the day now!

Week Nine

Day Fifty-Eight

Theme – I measure my progress step by step.

Quote – *Inspiration is for amateurs; achievers just show up and get to work. -Darren Hardy, Publisher, Success Magazine*

Question – Will you schedule at least one Power Hour this week? When?

Action – Record your action for the day now!

Week Nine

Day Fifty-Nine

Theme – I measure my progress step by step.

Quote – *It's amazing how people think four years is a long time to succeed in this business but think it's alright to stay broke at a job for 40 years. -Art Jonak*

Question – How will you track your activity?

Action – Record your action for the day now!

Week Nine

Day Sixty

Theme – I measure my progress step by step.

Quote – *Success is nothing more than a few simple disciplines practiced every day. -Jim Rohn*

Question – Who will you call to mentor you on the best income-producing activities for your business? Make the phone call.

Action – Record your action for the day now!

Week Nine

Day Sixty-One

Theme – I measure my progress step by step.

Quote – *Any success I've had in network marketing has come from a massive amount of compressed activity. -Matt Morris*

Question – Track your time today. What are you doing every hour? Where are you wasting time? Where are you productive?

Action – Record your action for the day now!

Week Nine

Day Sixty-Two

Theme – I measure my progress step by step.

Quote – *A work-at-home entrepreneur must be self-motivated, committed and willing to treat their business like a professional. Professionalism is an attitude, not a time commitment. -Deb Bixler, CashFlowShow.com*

Question – What activity will you add today to help boost your business?

Action – Record your action for the day now!

Week Nine

Day Sixty-Three

Theme – I measure my progress step by step.

Quote – *I don't know of many jobs where you stop working and they keep on paying you. -Todd Falcone, The Fearless Networker*

Question – What activities are bringing the greatest results for you?

Action – Record your action for the day now!

It's a Wrap! Week Nine

Passing the sixty day mark in your journey this week, you have certainly had positive and negative experiences along the way.

What have you learned from your failures or disappointments?

How has your attitude toward goal setting changed?

How will you adjust your daily actions for Week Ten?

Review your Action Path now. Review the steps again. As you work through the steps, add new items as necessary. Take the time now to assign your actions for Week Ten.

Week Ten

Connection - The Random

Week Ten

Focus for the Week - Connecting with the Cold Market (Yep! Complete Strangers)

Whether you are attending a networking group where you don't know a soul, going to your first PTA meeting at your child's new school, or reaching out to the cashier when you check out at the home improvement store, you can make a positive impression in a few short minutes. How will you create instant rapport with these strangers so they are curious about you?

First of all, let's be clear. You definitely do not lead with telling them about your business. Connecting with complete strangers is all about starting a relationship, not about making a sale. Your goal with a stranger is to get permission to reach out to them and secure their contact information.

Refining your rapport building skills will make connecting with people you have never met fun. You can turn it into a game! One of the most basic ways to connect with someone immediately is to determine their learning style. There are three basic learning styles. We all use all three styles. Yet everyone has a primary way they best assimilate information. Figure out someone's primary learning style then you can "speak their language" to connect with them instantly.

People like people who are like them. When you adapt your language and your tempo to match the person you are talking to, they feel much more connected to you. The primary learning styles are auditory, visual and feeling or touch. In a few moments, you can identify someone's primary learning style or preference of communication style by noticing the words they use and the tempo of their voice.

Primarily visual people tend to talk quickly. They use words that draw pictures for you such as focus, bright, imagine, clarity, watch, picture, examine, vivid and observe. Visuals will use phrases such as: How do you see yourself? Let me make this clear for you. Show me. I see what you are saying. We see eye to eye on this subject.

Auditory people tend to speak at an even pace. Words they use often include discuss, hear, sounds, click, speak, remark, say, speechless, tell, proclaim and resonate. From a primarily auditory person you might hear the phrases: I don't like your tone. Tell me more. I hear you. It sounds good to me. That rings a bell.

Touch or feeling-oriented people tend to speak more slowly. You will notice they use words to indicate what they are experiencing such as cold, connect, firm, pressure, share, make contact, feel, shocking and sharp. People who primarily experience life through touch or feeling will often use phrases like: I am calm, cool & collected. Shake it off. Stay in touch. The pressure is intense. How do you feel about that?

Determining the primary style of communicating for a stranger you meet will help you have rapport with them promptly. When you realize they are using visual words, then you can make a point to use visual words in what you are saying back to them. It helps them understand. If you notice they speak slowly, then slow down the tempo of your speaking to reflect their tempo. It will make them feel comfortable and connected to you.

Practice makes permanent. Start speaking to strangers more often. Practice listening and noticing what you believe is their primary learning and communication style. Build this muscle. Over time you want to be able to switch your tempo and words to naturally match others. Instant rapport is crucial for turning strangers into acquaintances, friends, referral sources and team members.

Since the goal is to secure their contact information (name and phone number--not just their email), you want to be in synch with them by having rapport when you ask. Look them in the eye, smile and ask. "Because you seem smart/motivated/happy/diligent, I would like to connect with you further. What is the best phone number for you?"

Week Ten

Day Sixty-Four

Theme – People are drawn to my great attitude.

Quote – *No matter how busy you are, you must take time to make the other person feel important. -Mary Kay Ash*

Question – What is your primary learning and communication style? What are words you use often?

Action – Record your action for the day now!

Week Ten

Day Sixty-Five

Theme – People are drawn to my great attitude.

Quote – *Talk less, listen more! Find out what the person wants and needs in their life and show them how they can achieve it! God gave you two ears and only one mouth. -Melynda Lilly, Network Marketing Professional*

Question – Think of your spouse or a close friend. What is their primary style? How will you communicate differently with them?

Action – Record your action for the day now!

Week Ten

Day Sixty-Six

Theme – People are drawn to my great attitude.

Quote – *Do what you say you're gonna do and people will follow you.*
-Lisa Grossman

Question – Where will you practice speaking with strangers today?

Action – Record your action for the day now!

Week Ten

Day Sixty-Seven

Theme – People are drawn to my great attitude.

Quote – *Direct sellers have the potential to make a huge difference in the world not just as a result of what thy sell but as a result of who they become. -Lyndsey Baigent, Party Plan Revolution*

Question – Where have you recently had a miscommunication? How would you handle it differently based on learning styles?

Action – Record your action for the day now!

Week Ten

Day Sixty-Eight

Theme – People are drawn to my great attitude.

Quote – *The doors will be opened to those who are bold enough to knock. –Tony Gaskins*

Question – How will you ask for a phone number? Write it out so you can practice in your voice and style.

Action – Record your action for the day now!

Week Ten

Day Sixty-Nine

Theme – People are drawn to my great attitude.

Quote – *Trust your hunches. They're usually based on facts filed away just below the conscious level. -Dr. Joyce Brothers*

Question – What group will you schedule to attend where you will meet strangers and practice building rapport? There are thousands of groups on MeetUp. Find one where you will be around people who have a common interest—walking, scrapbooking, biking, mystery lovers, etc.

Action – Record your action for the day now!

Week Ten

Day Seventy

Theme – People are drawn to my great attitude.

Quote – *Believe in yourself! Have faith in your abilities! Without a humble but reasonable confidence in your own powers you cannot be successful or happy. -Norman Vincent Peale*

Question – What feelings still come up for you when considering talking to strangers? How will you move away from those feelings toward confidence?

Action – Record your action for the day now!

It's a Wrap! Week Ten

Seventy days of persistent effort. Be proud. You have not given up!
Progress towards your outcome is important.

How has your business changed?

Who have you met that inspires you and why?

How will you adjust your daily actions for Week Eleven?

**Review your Action Path now. Review the steps again. As you
work through the steps, add new items as necessary. Take the
time now to assign your actions for Week Eleven.**

Week Eleven

Gratitude

Week Eleven

Focus for the Week - Gratitude

The words you speak become the house you live in. --Hafiz

In life you definitely get more of what you focus on. Are you constantly worrying or complaining? Do you take time each day to speak words of gratitude for what you have? Abundance is all around us, and yet, many people focus on what they don't have instead of the many blessings already present in their lives.

Having an attitude of gratitude improves your performance. Shawn Achor, Harvard Psychologist and author of *The Happiness Advantage*, has performed vast research on the relationship between happiness and success. Shawn purports if we study what is average, we will remain merely average. You will be what is considered normal. I highly recommend you listen to Shawn's
twelve minute TED Talk on Happiness.

Let's face it. Entrepreneurs are not normal. We also don't want to be average. We are stepping outside of our comfort zone to create extraordinary lives for ourselves. We don't want to be ordinary. If happiness leads to more success, we must choose to be happy. One of the best ways to raise your happiness quotient is to embrace gratitude.

How do you practice gratitude on a daily basis?

You can take five minutes when you awaken each morning, before getting out of bed, and list a few things you are grateful for in your life. Think of things that cannot be bought with money. Be very specific.

When you brush your teeth in the morning and evening, list for yourself three specific things you are grateful for in the last 24 hours. Be very specific.

Don't just say, I am grateful for a healthy family. Think of a family member and note what about their health you are grateful for today.

Up the ante, each day be sure your list of things you are grateful for does not include anything you have included on your list in the last week.

Keeping a gratitude journal is another practice to raise the level of joy in your life. Take a few moments each day to write down what you are grateful for in life. I actually use a ten-year journal as my gratitude journal. When you open the journal, each pair of pages has about six lines for you to write for that day each year. It is fascinating when I write for the current year to look at what I was grateful for on this exact day in years past.

Some days are hard. Maybe you aren't feeling overly grateful. Time to shake it off and face reality. Look around you. You have clothes, food, shelter, friends, water, and you are alive. Being grateful for what you have opens the space for more to come to you. When people focus on what they don't have, they create even more lack. Be grateful for what you do have and make space for even more abundance to come to you.

Another way to practice gratitude is to send notes to people you are grateful for in your life. I still send handwritten notes in the mail. Because receiving personal notes is so uncommon today, people really treasure the notes. You can also send personal emails. I schedule time in my calendar every Wednesday morning, and it is blocked off as "Gratitude Cards." Letting someone know you appreciate them definitely makes them feel good. It also reminds you the abundance of good people in your life.

Week Eleven

Day Seventy-One

Theme – Today I am grateful for my life.

Quote – *Do not be embarrassed by your failures, learn from them and start again. -Richard Branson*

Question – What are you grateful for today? Why?

Action – Record your action for the day now!

Week Eleven

Day Seventy-Two

Theme – Today I am grateful for my life.

Quote – *Discipline your disappointments. -Esther Spina, The Ambitious Woman*

Question – Who are you grateful for today? Why?

Action – Record your action for the day now!

Week Eleven

Day Seventy-Three

Theme – Today I am grateful for my life.

Quote – *Look for three things in a person—intelligence, energy and integrity. If they don't have the last one, don't even bother with the first two. -Warren Buffett*

Question – How will you express gratitude to someone today?

Action – Record your action for the day now!

Week Eleven

Day Seventy-Four

Theme – Today I am grateful for my life.

Quote – *Don't wish it was easier, wish you were better. Don't wish for less problems, wish for more skills. Don't wish for less challenge, wish for more wisdom. -Jim Rohn*

Question – What are you grateful for today? Why?

Action – Record your action for the day now!

Week Eleven

Day Seventy-Five

Theme – Today I am grateful for my life.

Quote – *If you have a positive attitude and constantly strive to give your best effort, eventually you will overcome your immediate problems and find you are ready for greater challenges. -Pat Riley*

Question – Who are you grateful for today? Why?

Action – Record your action for the day now!

Week Eleven

Day Seventy-Six

Theme – Today I am grateful for my life.

Quote – *I truly believe in positive synergy, that your positive mindset gives you a more hopeful outlook, and belief that you can do something great means you will do something great. -Russell Wilson*

Question – How will you express gratitude to someone today?

Action – Record your action for the day now!

Week Eleven

Day Seventy-Seven

Theme – Today I am grateful for my life.

Quote – *Far and away the best prize that life has to offer is the chance to work hard at work worth doing. -Teddy Roosevelt*

Question – What routine will you set up to regularly make your gratitude list?

Action – Record your action for the day now!

It's a Wrap! Week Eleven

Are there actions you know you should be taking toward your desired outcome that you are avoiding? You have a magical thirteen days remaining in this journey. Be courageous! Finish strongly!

What has been working for you?

What has not been working for you?

How will you adjust your daily actions for Week Twelve?

Review your Action Path now. Review the steps again. As you work through the steps, add new items as necessary. Take the time now to assign your actions for Week Twelve.

Week Twelve

Connection - The Giving

Week Twelve

Focus for the Week - The Giving

We are responsible to give back to the community we live it to make it better the next day. When I was a Girl Scout for nine years growing up, we were always taught to leave places better than we found them. If you have the ability to read this book, have shelter, sufficient food, clothes and transportation, you have privilege greater than many others on our globe. Therefore, in my opinion, you must give back to the community where you live. The community provides you a means to earn a living and build a business.

Opportunities abound to get involved and make a difference. You don't have to donate a million dollars or volunteer full-time to have an impact on the betterment of your community.

When Bob and I traveled to Hawaii for a couple of weeks, we enjoyed a fabulous week on Molokai in addition to our travels to Oahu and Kauai. Molokai is more rustic than many of the other islands. We enjoyed sunsets, black sand beaches and some great tennis matches. The only tennis court we could find was in a public park. The first day we played, we noticed all the trash in and around the court. On our second day to play, we brought trash bags and cleaned up the park before we played. On our last day to play, we left all the tennis balls we had brought with us for the youth who liked to use the court in the afternoons. Now we have traveled to fancy resorts where we pay a great deal to use their tennis courts. These public courts were free. We found a way to give back to the community while only being there for a week.

When was the last time you walked past a piece of trash without picking it up? Yes, picking up the trash is a small act and sometimes a little icky. And when you do it, you are bettering the world around you.

When you choose to get involved in a charitable cause, you have an impact in your community and meet other people who share your desire to change or improve what is going on with that cause. In addition, you meet people who are like you. Part of the art of connection is to be around people who share similar interests. Volunteering is good for your soul, blesses others and creates a new community of people for you to connect with.

You have the time because we all make time for what is most important to us. Even a couple of hours a month helping pack food at your local food bank. Gathering supplies for a domestic violence or homeless shelter. Reading to children after school. What touches your heart? Find a cause which moves you to action and make a point to get involved.

Reflect on who you will become in the process of giving back. I propose you will become a person others respect and admire. People will want to be around you even more and be part of what you are doing. As your business grows, also consider the financial contribution you will make to causes important to you.

> *You must be the change you wish to see in the world.*
> *-Mahatma Gandhi*

Week Twelve

Day Seventy-Eight

Theme – I naturally help others.

Quote – *Give what you want. Want courage? Encourage. Want hope? Give hope. Want love? Give love. Want success? Help someone else become successful. -Darren Hardy, Publisher, Success Magazine*

Question – How are you currently giving back to your community?

Action – Record your action for the day now!

Week Twelve

Day Seventy-Nine

Theme – I naturally help others.

Quote – *Communication—the human connection—is the key to personal and career success. -Paul J. Meyer*

Question – Who do you admire that is involved in volunteer work? How can you model them?

Action – Record your action for the day now!

Week Twelve

Day Eighty

Theme – I naturally help others.

Quote – *Never doubt that a small group of thoughtful, committed citizens can change the world; indeed, it's the only thing that ever has. -Margaret Mead*

Question – What one action will you do today to make a difference?

Action – Record your action for the day now!

Week Twelve

Day Eighty-One

Theme – I naturally help others.

Quote – *Always do your best. What you plant now, you will harvest later. -Og Mandino*

Question – How can you make a monetary donation today to impact your community or a cause important to you?

Action – Record your action for the day now!

Week Twelve

Day Eighty-Two

Theme – I naturally help others.

Quote – *Pretend that every single person you meet has a sign around his or her neck that says, "Make me feel important." Not only will you succeed in sales, you will succeed in life. -Mary Kay Ash*

Question – What type of people will you meet at a volunteer day? Find one coming up in the next few months in your community.

Action – Record your action for the day now!

Week Twelve

Day Eighty-Three

Theme – I naturally help others.

Quote – *Optimism is the faith that leads to achievement. Nothing can be done without hope and confidence. -Helen Keller*

Question – What random act of kindness will you do today? Pay for a stranger's coffee or lunch?

Action – Record your action for the day now!

Week Twelve

Day Eighty-Four

Theme – I naturally help others.

Quote – *Most of the important things in the world have been accomplished by people who have kept on trying when there seemed to be no hope at all. -Dale Carnegie*

Question – What emotions have you experienced by giving back?

Action – Record your action for the day now!

It's a Wrap! Week Twelve

Come on, you must be madly impressed with yourself! With a handful of days remaining in your 90-day plan, you can measure the progress, recount all the learning experiences and celebrate. Focus for these last six days.

Where do you feel more confident in your business skills?

How will you celebrate and reward yourself for completing the 90 days?

How will you adjust your daily actions for Week Thirteen?

Review your Action Path now. Review the steps again. As you work through the steps, add new items as necessary. Take the time now to assign your actions for Week Thirteen.

Week Thirteen

Awareness & Celebration

Week Thirteen

Focus for the Week - Awareness & Celebration

Our final week.

You are in the home stretch and you have learned so much about yourself and your business. Even when you were struggling to make each day happen, you stuck with it. You are now very aware that you CAN make things happen and you CAN succeed no matter how difficult it is. No matter what you do in your life now, this awareness will serve you throughout your life.

Living in a state of awareness allows you to continuously grow and redefine yourself. You have built the skill of observing yourself and shifting your behaviors to achieve your business outcomes. This skill can and should be used in all the areas of your life. Embrace it. It will serve you well.

During this last stretch, enjoy each and every moment of it. Celebrate with enthusiasm. Finish strong and happy.

You deserve every moment of greatness.

Week Thirteen

Day Eighty-Five

Theme – I am the master of my days!

Quote – *A great leader knows their job is to help others. They are "other people" centered and have a heart for helping others achieve their goals and dreams. -Teresa Garrison, The Success Factory*

Question – How are you feeling about your accomplishments today?

Action – Record your action for the day now!

Week Thirteen

Day Eighty-Six

Theme – I am the master of my days!

Quote – *The worst thing you can do in this economy is to get a second job! The best thing you can do is begin a home-based business. –Dave Ramsey*

Question – What character trait has shown up for you during this 90 days that you didn't realize was prevalent in your life?

Action – Record your action for the day now!

Week Thirteen

Day Eighty-Seven

Theme – I am the master of my days!

Quote – *If your actions inspire others to dream more, learn more, do more and become more, you are a leader. -John Quincy Adams*

Question – Who have you attracted into your life because of your commitment?

Action – Record your action for the day now!

Week Thirteen

Day Eighty-Eight

Theme – I am the master of my days!

Quote – *My mission in life is not merely to survive, but to thrive; and to do so with some passion, some compassion, some humor and some style. -Maya Angelou*

Question – What habits have you created during this process?

Action – Record your action for the day now!

Week Thirteen

Day Eighty-Nine

Theme – I am the master of my days!

Quote – *It does not matter how slowly you go as long as you do not stop. -Confucius*

Question – When will you schedule your 90 day reward?

Action – Record your action for the day now!

Week Thirteen

Day Ninety

Theme – I am the master of my days!

Quote – You do not attract what you want. You attract who you are.
-Dr. Wayne Dyer

Question – Who are you showing up as today?

Action – Record your action for the day now!

It's a Wrap! 90 Days!

We are giving you a standing ovation from afar! You completed your journey. You have made measured progress toward your outcome. Let's take a little time of reflection

How do you now describe your attitude towards your business?

How have you changed as a leader?

What new connections exist in your life, and how will they benefit you?

Are you practicing gratitude? What impact does this ritual have on your daily mindset?

How are you thriving in your business?

What self-care practices have you established?

What did you learn about yourself which will help you be a better leader?

What's next for you?

Thank You.

You have spent the last 90 days with us on this journey. We are thrilled and proud that you made it the point!

No matter what you have accomplished, making the commitment and taking the journey with your business is at the heart of all the lessons. Sometimes we have success and sometimes we fail, however, the way we show up during the journey is what matters. Be confident! Maybe it is time to lead your team on a 90 day journey. Imagine the results not only to your income but to the environment and mindset of your team when they reach the 90 days of action

You have done what most will never even attempt. It was not easy. It was not quick. It did not involve instant gratification. You still did it. We have been right there with you and we understand what it took to get here. Celebrate the person you have become and the business you have now grown. Whether you reached your desired outcome or not, stand proudly and confidently in front of your team. The lesson was in making the commitment. The person you became during this journey is what truly matters.

You are on your way to making a difference in your company, with your team members, family & friends. May your business flourish as you continue to grow. We are ready for another 90 day journey when you are!

Remember, always find a way to enjoy the entire journey, moment to moment.

Huge big hugs and much love to you,
Kim & Alice

www.NailItIn90.com

www.ingramcontent.com/pod-product-compliance
Lightning Source LLC
Chambersburg PA
CBHW051335200326

41519CB00026B/7437